speak out 2ND EDITION

Pre-intermediate
Workbook

T0385819

Antonia Clare • JJ Wilson
Damian Williams

CONTENTS

CONTENTS

VOCABULARY

FREE TIME

1 Match phrases 1–10 with pictures A–J.

1 go shopping _____
2 go on holiday _____
3 spend time with family _____
4 spend money _____
5 eat out _____
6 eat with friends _____
7 have time off _____
8 have a barbecue _____
9 play volleyball _____
10 play the guitar _____

A

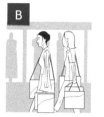
B

C

D

E

F

G

H

I

J

GRAMMAR

QUESTION FORMS

2 Put the words in the correct order to make questions.

1 is / birthday / when / your?
   When is your birthday?

2 English / time / lessons / your / start / what / do?
   _____

3 friends / cook for / often / you / how / your / do?
   _____

4 in / many / family / how / are / your / people?
   _____

5 come / does / mother / where / your / from?
   _____

6 sell / you / did / why / house / your?
   _____

7 glasses / in / of / many / day / water / you / how / drink / a / do?
   _____

8 is / where / the / classroom?
   _____

9 your / best / see / did / friend / when / last / you?
   _____

10 go / shopping / where / did / you?
   _____

3 Write questions for the answers. Use the question words in the box.

where	what	why	when	who	how often
which	how many	what			

1 A: *Where are you from* ?
   B: I'm from Poland.

2 A: _____ ?
   B: I'm a student.

3 A: _____ with?
   B: I live with my friend Olga.

4 A: _____ ?
   B: Only two people live in the house, Olga and me.

5 A: _____ ?
   B: In our free time we like to go to the cinema or go out with friends. We both love reading, too.

6 A: _____ ?
   B: We go to the cinema about once a week.

7 A: _____ ?
   B: I'm studying English because I would like to work in this country.

8 A: _____ – 2A or 3A?
   B: I'm in class 2A, Pre-intermediate.

9 A: _____ ?
   B: I started learning English when I was at school.

READING

4 A Read the article and match headings A–F with paragraphs 1–6.

A Call a friend
B Just smile
C Do something nice for someone
D Be active
E Do that difficult job
F Plan for some future fun

MAKE YOURSELF HAPPY!

Six tips to make you happier in the next hour

You can make yourself happier starting now. In the next hour, do as many of these things as possible. Each thing you do will help you to feel happier.

1 _____: stand up and walk around while you talk on the phone. Or go for a quick ten-minute walk outside. Doing exercise gives you energy and makes you feel better.

2 _____: arrange to meet someone for lunch or send an email to a friend you haven't seen for a long time. Having good relationships with other people is one of the things that makes us happy, so stay in touch with your friends.

3 _____: answer a difficult email or call to make that dentist's appointment. Do it now, don't wait. Cross something off your list of things to do, to give yourself energy.

4 _____: order a book you want to read, plan a trip to a museum or a night out with friends. If you look forward to doing something fun in the future, it will make you feel happy right now.

5 _____: buy someone flowers, carry their bag, tell them they look nice. Do good, feel good – this really works. If you do something nice for someone, it makes you feel better.

6 _____: even when you don't feel happy, always try to smile. Put a smile on your face right now – it will make you feel better!

Tick things off the list when you do them. Do you feel happier yet?

Tick things off the list when you do them. Do you feel happier yet?

B Read the article again. Are the sentences true (T) or false (F)?

1 Doing exercise makes you tired. _____
2 Having friends is an important part of being happy. _____
3 Doing a difficult job uses all your energy. _____
4 Planning fun things to do can make you feel happy. _____
5 If you do something to make someone else feel good, you will feel good yourself. _____
6 Smiling when you're not happy can make you feel bad. _____

C Read the article again and answer the questions.

1 What should you do when you talk on the phone?
_____

2 Why is it important to stay in touch with friends?
_____

3 What kinds of jobs are on a 'things to do' list?
_____

4 Why is it a good idea to organise something fun to do in the future?
_____

5 How will you feel if you buy someone flowers or carry their bag?
_____

6 What happens when you smile?
_____

D Complete the definitions with words from the article.

1 do _____: do some kind of activity like walking or playing tennis
2 have good _____ with people: be friendly with people
3 stay in _____ with people: contact people regularly (by phone, email, etc.)
4 _____ something off a list: mark things on a list when you do them
5 look _____ to something: be excited about something which will happen in the future

VOCABULARY
RELATIONSHIPS

1 Look at the pictures and complete the story about when Harry met Sally. Use the words in the box.

| proposed got engaged ~~have a girlfriend~~ met |
| got married accepted got on well fell in love |

1 Harry didn't
have a girlfriend.

2 He _____
Sally in a café.
They _____.

3 They _____.

4 He _____ to her
and she _____.
They _____.

5 They _____.

GRAMMAR
PAST SIMPLE

2 A Mark the verbs in the box regular (R) or irregular (I).

| fall I ask decide know stop like go say |
| see spend study try meet walk work get |

B Write the past simple form of the irregular verbs in Exercise 2A.

3 Complete the story with the past simple form of the verbs in the box.

| become decide meet send get propose |
| have not tell start arrive live talk |

Many years ago, before it was fashionable to date on the internet, I ^{1}_____ a Swedish lady online. We ^{2}_____ on well from the first minute we ^{3}_____ chatting, and she soon ^{4}_____ my girlfriend. The only problem was that I ^{5}_____ in the UK and she was in Sweden. For a couple of years, we ^{6}_____ a long-distance relationship. We ^{7}_____ on the phone and ^{8}_____ emails to each other. We ^{9}_____ our friends how we met because we were embarrassed. After a while, I ^{10}_____ to leave England and move to Sweden. When I ^{11}_____, I ^{12}_____ to her and she said yes. Now, we are happily married and we have four children. I think online dating is fantastic. I met my wife because of it!

4 Complete the sentences with the past simple form of the verbs in brackets.

1 A: Where _____ (you/stay)?
   B: We _____ (find) a hotel near the station.
2 We _____ (eat) in the hotel restaurant and the food _____ (be) delicious.
3 Mara and Steve _____ (not have) a barbecue on Sunday because it _____ (rain) all day.
4 We _____ (go) to the cinema, but I _____ (not like) the film. I _____ (think) it was really boring.
5 I _____ (spend) the weekend studying because I've got an exam tomorrow.
6 He _____ (be) really busy yesterday, so he _____ (not have) time to call you.
7 She _____ (write) a long letter explaining the problem, but her boyfriend still _____ (not understand).
8 They _____ (give) her some beautiful flowers for her birthday.
9 A: What time _____ (you/get) back home last night?
   B: At about midnight.
10 I _____ (start) this job four years ago, when I _____ (move) to Rome.

5 A Say the words and circle the verb ending which sounds different.

1 played	stayed	tried	ended
2 asked	kissed	arrived	talked
3 finished	decided	pretended	wanted
4 studied	happened	invented	stayed
5 walked	helped	stopped	started

B ▶ 1.1 Listen and check.

LISTENING

6 A ▶ 1.2 Listen to Chris's story of how he met Amy. Number the sentences in the correct order.

a) Chris met Amy in Spain.   _____

b) Chris met Amy in London.   _____

c) Chris went on holiday with his friends. _____

d) They got married and had a son.   _____

e) They decided to stop writing to each other. _____

f) They fell in love.   _____

B Listen again and answer the questions.

1 How old was Chris when he met Amy?

_____

2 Where were they?

_____

3 What did they promise to do after the holiday?

_____

4 Why did they decide to stop writing to each other?

_____

5 When did they meet again?

_____

6 How did they feel when they saw each other?

_____

7 What's their son's name?

_____

C Read audio script 1.2 on page 77 and find words that match these meanings.

1 friends _____

2 lying in the sun _____

3 knew who somebody was when you saw them

_____

4 very surprised _____

5 spending time with someone

_____

WRITING

LINKING WORDS

7 Correct the linking words in *italics* in the sentences.

because

1 I didn't like the film / *so* it was scary.

2 We saw Pompeii *but* we thought it was wonderful.

3 She didn't like her job, *because* she decided to leave.

4 They couldn't get married *and* her father wouldn't allow it.

5 He started taekwondo lessons *but* he wanted to get fit.

6 They wanted to buy the house, *so* the bank didn't give them the money.

7 I wanted to go to the concert, *because* I couldn't find a ticket.

8 I didn't sleep very well, *but* I'm very tired today.

8 Join the sentences. Use *and*, *so*, *but* or *because*.

1 We decided to sell the car. We needed the money.
   We decided to sell the car because we needed the money.

2 Jon met Ella in an online group. They got on really well.

_____

3 I didn't want to be late. I left home early.

_____

4 Matt proposed to Fiona. She said no.

_____

5 I like Clara. She can be a bit rude sometimes.

_____

6 We got married two years ago. We had a baby a year later.

_____

7 The film was terrible. They left early.

_____

8 I'm studying medicine. I want to be a doctor.

_____

VOCABULARY
CONVERSATION TOPICS

1 **A** Find six verbs in the puzzle.

G	O	S	S	I	P	T
D	F	A	S	N	R	K
W	E	Y	L	T	S	D
Q	H	R	T	E	L	L
W	J	E	E	R	G	T
T	T	S	A	R	I	I
H	A	V	E	U	O	U
H	L	V	G	P	S	T
R	K	S	U	T	I	L

B Complete the sentences with verbs from Exercise 1A. Use one of the verbs twice.

1 We often _____ interesting conversations in our English class.
2 You shouldn't _____ so much about people at work. It's not very nice.
3 You look sad. Shall I you _____ a joke?
4 What did your mum _____ when you got home late last night?
5 So, Judy, _____ me about your new job.
6 What did you _____ about with your sister last night?
7 Why do you always _____ me when I'm in the middle of a story? I hate that!

FUNCTION
MAKING CONVERSATION

2 Complete the conversations with the words and phrases in the box.

> do you   work here   see you   did you
> I'm sorry   my friend   isn't it   was terrible
> would you   good weekend

1 A: Hi, Helen. This is _____ Joshua.
  B: Hi, Joshua. Pleased to meet you.
2 A: Did you have a _____?
  B: Yes, thanks. I didn't do much.
3 A: Nice day, _____?
  B: Yes, it's lovely.
4 A: So, do you _____?
  B: No, I'm just visiting.
5 A: _____ like a drink?
  B: Thanks. I'd love a glass of water.
6 A: _____ watch the film last night?
  B: Yes. It was brilliant.
7 A: Where exactly _____ come from?
  B: I'm from Bolton, near Manchester.
8 A: Sorry I'm late. I had some bad news at home.
  B: Oh, _____ to hear that.
9 A: Did you watch the match last night?
  B: Yes, it _____!
10 A: I'll see you later.
  B: Yes, _____ soon.

LEARN TO
SOUND NATURAL

3 ▶ 1.3 Listen and mark the linked words.
  1 Do‿you like‿it here?
  2 Where are you going?
  3 I come from Italy.
  4 It's a beautiful day.
  5 I'm afraid I can't remember.
  6 Where did you buy it?
  7 I'm sorry, but I don't understand.

4 ▶ 1.4 Listen and write what you hear.
  1 _____
  2 _____
  3 _____
  4 _____
  5 _____
  6 _____

2 WORK

VOCABULARY

WORK

1 Read the clues and complete the puzzle. What's the mystery word?

1 a business that makes or sells things or provides services
2 extra money a worker gets
3 everyone who works in a company
4 a job you have to do
5 a person who manages the workers
6 someone who works for a business
7 a place where many people work at desks
8 money you get regularly when you do a job

```
              ¹C  O  M  P  A  N  Y
     ²□□□□□□
              ³□□□□□□
              ⁴□□□□□
       ⁵□□□□
       ⁶□□□□□□□
 ⁷□□□□□□□
       ⁸□□□□□□
```

Mystery word: _____

GRAMMAR

PRESENT SIMPLE AND CONTINUOUS

2 Match the sentence halves.

1 a) I'm doing my homework,   _____
  b) I do my homework   _____
  i) on the bus most days.
  ii) so I can't come to the party with you.

2 a) I'm not enjoying this film –   _____
  b) I don't enjoy films –
  i) can we watch the other DVD?
  ii) I prefer reading.

3 a) I'm looking for   _____
  b) I look for
  i) new artists. It's an interesting job.
  ii) Maria. Have you seen her?

4 a) I'm standing   _____
  b) I stand
  i) on the bridge every day and watch the boats.
  ii) on the bridge. I can see you!

5 a) The train is arriving   _____
  b) The train arrives   _____
  i) late sometimes.
  ii) in London now. See you in five minutes.

6 a) Are you using   _____
  b) Do you use   _____
  i) this pen? No? OK, I'll use it for amoment.
  ii) a pen and paper or do you do everything on the computer?

3 Complete the conversations with the present simple or present continuous form of the verbs in brackets.

1 A: Why _____ (you/smile)?
  B: Ahmed just told me a very funny joke!

2 A: How many people _____ (you/know) here?
  B: No one except you!

3 A: Did you hear that noise next door?
  B: Yes! What _____ they/do)?

4 A: What _____ (you/drink)?
  B: Apple juice. But I don't want any more, thanks.

5 A: _____ (he/be) an actor?
  B: No, that's his famous twin brother.

6 A: Which one is Sharon?
  B: _____ (she/wear) the blue dress.

4 A Complete the text with the present simple or present continuous form of the verbs in brackets.

" Here are some photos of my new friends. This is Amei. She ¹_____ (be) an artist, but at the moment she ²_____ (work) as a teacher. She ³_____ (not like) teaching very much! And this is Bruce, her husband. This is Hernan. He's from Santiago, Chile. He ⁴_____ (be) a maths teacher, but he ⁵_____ (do) his Master's in education in the USA at the moment. In the photo he ⁶_____ (smile) because he passed an exam that day! This is Julio from Colombia. He ⁷_____ (have) a job in an oil company. In the picture he ⁸_____ (play) his guitar – he's really good! The other picture is Natasha from Trinidad. She graduated last year and she ⁹_____ (look) for a job. Her parents ¹⁰_____ (visit) her at the moment. "

B Read the text again and label the people in the pictures.

1 _____

2 _____

3 _____

4 _____

5 _____

READING

5 A Read the article and choose the best summary.
1 how one company keeps its workers happy
2 things that companies do to motivate their workers
3 working for the world's best companies

FUN AT WORK

Are they great ideas or just crazy? Here are some ways that companies keep their employees happy.

1 **Sport can be a good way for busy workers to relax.** Wright, Newman & Fischer, a group of lawyers based in London, has a small golf course in the office. The first part of the course is on the fifth floor. When your ball drops down the ninth hole, the course continues on the fourth floor. An even more relaxing sport is bowling. Maybe this is why a company called Permatech has a complete bowling alley in the basement. The employees go bowling after work and really enjoy it.

2 **What about alternatives to boring suits and company uniforms?** One company has 'fancy-dress Fridays'. On the last Friday of every month, each department chooses a theme and the workers dress up accordingly. One department came as famous actors, with the boss dressed as Brad Pitt. Another department chose historical figures; there were three Julius Caesars and two Genghis Khans! And how about this idea from a company called LineHut, in Paris: they hold moustache-growing competitions for employees and customers! For men only, of course!

3 **Some companies like to take their employees out of the office.** Finchley Management takes its workers on a trip every year. The workers go to the airport, but they don't know what country they are flying to! Trips in the past have included Rio de Janeiro, Bangkok and the Bahamas. In another company, Wicked Shakes, the staff go on free skiing holidays. And if workers stay with the US-based Indulgence Swiss Chocolate Company for five years, they get a free trip to Switzerland to taste the chocolate!

B Read the text again and answer the questions.
1 Where exactly is the golf course at Wright, Newman & Fischer?
_____
2 How can the employees at Permatech relax after work?
_____
3 What are 'fancy-dress Fridays'?
_____
4 What surprise do the employees of Finchley Management get every year?
_____

C Find words in the article that match these meanings.
1 a place where you can go bowling (paragraph 1)
_____
2 a room in a building that is below the level of the ground (paragraph 1)
_____
3 other possibilities (paragraph 2)
_____
4 clothes that everyone in a company or group wears (paragraph 2)
_____
5 important or famous people from the past (paragraph 2)
_____
6 a visit to a place (paragraph 3)
_____

WRITING

AN EMAIL

6 A Underline the correct alternatives. Which email is formal? Which is informal?

> [1]*Dear/Hi* Mr Yevgeny,
> I am writing [2]*about/for* the advertisement for a hotel cleaner that I saw in Jobs Monthly. I have attached my CV.
> I look forward to [3]*hear/hearing* from you.
> [4]*Yours sincerely/Bye for now,*
> Milly Clapton

> [5]*Bye/Hi* Dave,
> [6]*It's/There's* about the party. Can you bring your laptop and some MP3s?
> [7]*See/Speak* you soon.
> [8]*Yours sincerely/Cheers,*
> Elena

B Your company has decided to have 'fancy-dress Fridays'. Write a formal email to your colleagues (50–100 words). Include the information below.
1 Say what you are writing about.
2 Explain what 'fancy-dress Fridays' are.
3 Invite ideas for fancy dress.

VOCABULARY

JOBS

1 Who's talking? Match the jobs in the box with what the people say.

> ~~motorcycle courier~~   sales rep   fashion designer
> foreign correspondent   personal trainer
> IT consultant   rescue worker

1 'The biggest problem in my job is the number of cars in the city.'   _motorcycle courier_

2 'I like my job because I travel the world and see important events.' _____

3 'We believe in making clothes for normal people, not only for beautiful models.'

_____

4 'In my job, you need to love computers and technology.' _____

5 'In my team, we save about ten lives a year.'

_____

6 'My job is easier when I like the product that I'm trying to sell.' _____

7 'I like helping people to get stronger and fitter.'

_____

2 A Look at the jobs in Exercise 1 again. How many syllables does each job have? Write the job next to the number of syllables.

7 syllables: _____ _motorcycle courier_ _____

6 syllables: _____

5 syllables: _____ , _____ , _____

4 syllables: _____

2 syllables: _____

B Underline the stressed syllables in the words in Exercise 2A.

C ▶ 2.1 Listen and check.

3 Complete the job advertisements with the words in the box.

> team   holidays   salary   ~~deal~~   with   pressure   risk

— IT CONSULTANT —

needed for six-month contract in Abu Dhabi. You will need to [1] _____deal_____ with IT problems in the head office at Magran James Manufacturers. You must be good at working in a [2] _____ and working under [3] _____ .
Benefits: very good [4] _____ ($240,000, tax-free) and excellent conditions. House provided.

If you want a job with long [5] _____ , come and speak to **Safari Travel Inc**. We are looking for qualified **safari guides**. You don't need to [6] _____ your life fighting lions and crocodiles, but you must know about outdoor living and be good at dealing [7] _____ customers.
Call the number below for more information.

0802 276 6671

GRAMMAR

ADVERBS OF FREQUENCY

4 A Underline the correct alternatives to complete the quotes.

1 'People who work sitting down _always_/_never_ get paid more than people who work standing up.'

2 'The successful people are _occasionally_/_usually_ the ones who listen more than they talk.'

3 'Politicians _always_/_never_ believe what they say, so they are surprised when other people do.'

4 '_Once in a while_/_Usually_ teachers will open a door, if you're lucky, but you have to enter alone.'

5 'Great artists like van Gogh _rarely_/_sometimes_ live to see their success.'

6 'Doctors are the same as lawyers. The only difference is that lawyers rob you, but doctors rob you _and_ kill you _occasionally_/_usually_.'

7 'Find something you love doing and you'll _sometimes_/_never_ have to work a day in your life.'

8 'The only place where success _hardly ever_/_always_ comes before work is in the dictionary.'

B ▶ 2.2 Listen and check.

5 A What do these people think about accidents? Read the quotes and complete the sentences with the words in the box and _happen_.

> ~~hardly ever~~   never   rarely   often

1 'My job is really safe. In twenty years, I've only heard of one accident.' (estate agent)
Accidents _____ _hardly ever happen_ _____ .

2 'Bad accidents happen once every two or three years.' (plumber)
Accidents _____ .

3 'It's a very dangerous job. A lot of people die.' (fisherman)
Accidents _____ .

4 'We have a completely safe job. The only danger is to your eyes from reading too much!' (university lecturer)
Accidents _____ .

B What do these people think about accidents? Read the quotes and complete the sentences with the words in the box and _happen_.

> once in a while   occasionally   always

1 'In ten years I've heard about one or two accidents when animals have attacked.' (vet)
Accidents _____ .

2 'Danger is part of the job. When you work with guns, accidents happen every day.' (soldier)
Accidents _____ .

3 'Three or four times a year there are serious accidents.' (electrician)
Accidents _____ .

LISTENING

6 A Label the picture with the words in the box.

> tour bus   safari guide   tourists   male elephant   pool

1 _____tour bus_____

3 _____

4 _____

2 _____

5 _____

B ▶ **2.3** Listen to two people talking about what happened in the picture. Answer the questions.

1 Who is speaking in each story?

_____

2 Why was it a frightening experience?

_____

3 What happened in the end? Was anyone injured?

_____

C Read the sentences. Are they from Story 1 or Story 2? Listen again to check.

1 I had a bus full of tourists. There were fifteen of them.   _Story 1_

2 There were twenty of us tourists.   _Story 2_

3 It was a beautiful, clear evening and about seven o'clock we saw some elephants.   _____

4 One evening, at about six o'clock, we went for a drive in the tour bus.   _____

5 I told the tourists to walk very slowly back to the bus.   _____

6 [He] told us to run back to the bus as fast as possible.   _____

D Circle the correct meaning for the phrases in bold.

1 They could **get off the bus**.
   a) stay on the bus
   b) leave the bus

2 The elephant **charged at us**.
   a) ran at us very fast
   b) looked at us and made a loud noise

3 The tourists were **screaming**.
   a) making a loud noise because they were frightened
   b) getting angry

4 I started driving **as fast as possible**.
   a) not very quickly
   b) very quickly

E Read audio script 2.3 on page 77 and check your answers.

FUNCTION
EXPRESSING LIKES/DISLIKES

1 A Complete the sentences with the words in the box.

don't   on   absolutely   can't
very   love   mind   keen

1 I'm very _____ on cooking and I _____ love great food.

2 I _____ riding my motorbike. I _____ stand sitting in an office all day.

3 I'm quite keen _____ technology and I don't _____ dealing with other people's computer problems.

4 I'm _____ keen on working with money and I _____ like people wasting it on stupid things.

B ▶ 2.4 Listen and check.

C Match jobs a)–d) with sentences 1–4 in Exercise 1A.

a) accountant   _____
b) chef   _____
c) IT consultant   _____
d) motorcycle courier _____

2 A Put the words in the correct order to make sentences.

1 like / team / you / a / do / in / working?
_____

2 working / can't / pressure / I / stand / under
_____

3 my / not / I'm / very / on / boss / keen
_____

4 colleagues / don't / my / like / I
_____

5 dealing / don't / customers / I / mind / with
_____

6 keen / sport / you / on / are?
_____

B Match responses a)–f) with sentences 1–6 in Exercise 2A.

a) Why? What's wrong with her?   _____
b) I'm not surprised. They don't seem very friendly.   _____
c) That's good because it's important for a sales assistant.   _____
d) I love it, especially football.   _____
e) Why? Do you get stressed?   _____
f) Yes, I do. Actually, I hate working alone.   _____

VOCABULARY
TYPES OF WORK

3 Match sentences 1–8 with types of work A–H.

1 I deal with the money that goes in and out of the company.   _A_
2 I prepare fresh sandwiches for our customers.   _____
3 I design clothes.   _____
4 I teach teenagers maths and science.   _____
5 I organise advertising for the company's products and speak to customers.   _____
6 I show people all the best places to visit and things to do in my city.   _____
7 I act in films and in the theatre.   _____
8 I work in a shop, selling products to our customers.   _____

A works in accounts   **B** works in retail
C works in education   **D** works in sales and marketing
E works in the fashion industry
F works in the entertainment industry
G works in the tourist industry
H works in the food industry

LEARN TO
RESPOND AND ASK MORE QUESTIONS

4 A Complete the words in the conversations.

Conversation 1
A: On Saturday I went to a conference about the Z-phone, this amazing new technology.
B: [1]R__ lly? I read about that last week. It [2]s__ __nds __nt__r__st__ng.
A: Well, everybody's talking about it.
B: [3]__nd wh__t __b__ __t the cost?
A: Oh, I don't know. I had to leave before they discussed that.

Conversation 2
A: Today I was offered a job as a babysitter.
B: [4]Th__t's gr__ __t!
A: Not really. They only offered me five pounds an hour.
B: Oh, I [5]s__ __. So did you accept the job?
A: No. I'm going to look for something better.
B: [6]R__ ght. What did you tell them?
A: I said, 'Dad, I know the baby is my sister, but I want a better salary!'

B ▶ 2.5 Listen and check.

C ▶ 2.6 Listen and repeat B's responses. Notice the intonation. Copy the intonation to sound interested.

VOCABULARY

TIME OUT

1 Complete the sentences with verbs.

1 I'm going to ____see____ a jazz band tonight. My sister says they're really good.

2 I usually _____ the bus to work because it's easy and it's cheap.

3 We like to _____ to a museum at the weekend. You can learn new things and it's better than watching television.

4 Did you _____ the photographic exhibition in the Sainsbury Centre? It was brilliant.

5 I'm really hungry. Can we stop and _____ a snack from this café?

6 We're going to _____ a drink in the bar later. Do you want to meet us there?

7 I really want to _____ dancing. I haven't been for ages!

8 Why don't we _____ sightseeing? We can spend the whole day walking around the city.

9 Where do you want to _____ dinner? There's a nice restaurant around the corner.

GRAMMAR

PRESENT CONTINUOUS/*BE GOING TO* FOR FUTURE

2 A Put the words in the correct order to make questions.

1 going / holiday / are / you / away / year / this / on?

_____

2 is / dinner / evening / who / your / cooking / this?

_____

3 are / going / to / dentist / when / the / you?

_____

4 weekend / are / this / doing / you / what?

_____

5 play / are / sport / you / to / this / any / going / week?

_____

6 you / marry / are / to / going / Roberto?

_____

7 what / meeting / you / time / your / are / sister?

_____

8 are / to / English / do / your / what / improve / going / you / to?

_____

9 you / a / the / are / party / at / weekend / having?

_____

10 gym / work / are / to / the / you / after / going?

_____

B Match answers a)–j) with questions 1–10 in Exercise 2A.

a) Nobody. I'm just going to eat some salad and fruit.   __2__

b) Six o'clock. We're going out for a meal.   _____

c) Yes, we're getting married in the summer.   _____

d) I'm going to read as much as possible in English.   _____

e) Next Tuesday – in the morning.   _____

f) No. I'm going to Greece next summer, but I'm not going anywhere this year.   _____

g) Yes, I'm playing tennis with Jim on Friday.   _____

h) Some friends are coming to stay, so we're taking them up to the mountains.   _____

i) No, I'm going out for dinner.   _____

j) Yes, do you want to come?   _____

3 Complete the conversations with the phrases in the box.

are you coming   going to look for   are you going
'm speaking   are you doing   're going
are meeting   'm staying

1 A: Hi, Boris. What _____ later?
   B: Nothing much. I _____ at home tonight.

2 A: What are your plans for the summer?
   B: I'm _____ a job.

3 A: Have you seen Anita?
   B: No, but I _____ to her later.

4 A: When does your brother arrive?
   B: My parents _____ him at the station at 6.30p.m.

5 A: _____ to the party on Saturday?
   B: I'm not sure. I haven't been invited.

6 A: Where _____ for your holiday?
   B: We _____ cycling in the Netherlands.

THREE THINGS TO DO IN ... NEW YORK

There are so many things to see and do in New York, sometimes it's difficult to know where to start. In this week's guide, we look at three things you can't miss when you visit the city.

Start by spending some time in Central Park. With over 25,000 trees and lots of different types of birds, it's easy to forget you're in a big city. Relax and enjoy the fresh air or go for a tour in a horse and carriage. In summer you can go out on the lake in a boat or kayak, and in winter you can go ice-skating! After all that activity you'll be hungry, so have lunch at the famous Tavern on the Green. Great concerts take place in Central Park, too. Every year the New York Philharmonic Orchestra gives a free open-air concert and there's also the New York Shakespeare Festival at the theatre in the park.

They say that Paris has the Eiffel Tower, London has the London Eye and New York has the Empire State Building. But many people think the best views of the city are from the 'Top of the Rock' – the top floor of the GE (General Electric) building, a skyscraper in the middle of the city. At 260 metres high, it's the fourteenth tallest building in New York, and from the top you can have a fantastic view of the city.

Many people visit the famous Statue of Liberty by ferry, but also on the way is the Immigration Museum on Ellis Island. This was the place where people first arrived from 1892 to 1954, many after a long and difficult journey from other countries. Most of the island is closed to the general public, but you can visit the museum and find out about the many people who arrived here. You can also go on a tour with a guide to visit some of the old, unused buildings on the island. A very interesting day out for everyone.

READING

4 A Read the article and complete the sentences with a name or a number.

1 There are more than _____ trees in Central Park.
2 The famous restaurant in Central Park is called the _____.
3 Every year, the New York _____ Festival has plays in the park.
4 The top floor of the GE building is called the '_____'.
5 On Ellis island you can visit the _____ Museum.
6 People from other countries started arriving on Ellis Island in _____.

B Read the article again and answer the questions.

1 Why is it 'easy to forget you're in a big city' when you visit Central Park?

_____

2 What can you do in Central Park in winter?

_____

3 What is the GE building?

_____

4 How do you get to Ellis Island and the Statue of Liberty?

_____

5 What else, apart from the museum, can you visit on Ellis island?

_____

WRITING

INVITATIONS

5 Find and correct eight grammatical mistakes in the messages.

> Hi Mike,
> *I'm playing*
> ~~I play~~ football later with a few of the boys from work. Would you like to coming?
> Dan

> Dan,
> I'm sorry, but I busy tonight. I take Leila out for a meal. Wish me luck!
> Thanks anyway.
> Mike

> Hi guys,
> A few of us is going out for a curry on Friday night. Do you want come with us? We're meet at the Indian Tree at 8p.m.
> Emma

> Hi Emma,
> I love to. See you there.
> Jan

6 A Complete the invitations using the prompts.

> 1 _____
> (I / have / party) at my house on Saturday.
> 2 _____
> (you / want / come)?
> 3 _____
> (we / go / have / music) and plenty of food. Bring your friends too. Just let me know.
> Kristoph

> 4 _____
> (Julie / get / tickets / for / theatre) next Wednesday.
> 5 _____
> (we go / see / Shakespeare's *Hamlet*).
> 6 _____
> (would / like / come)? The tickets are £17.50.
> Becca

B Write your own answers to the emails in Exercise 6A, explaining why you would like to/can't come. Write 50–100 words.

VOCABULARY

PLACES TO VISIT

1 A Match 1–8 with a)–h) to make compound nouns. Then write them in the spaces below. Which compound nouns are two words? Which are one word?

1 night   a) field
2 shopping   b) front
3 water   c) hall
4 nature   d) club
5 concert   e) trail
6 street   f) side
7 sports   g) market
8 country   h) mall

1 _____   5 _____
2 _____   6 _____
3 _____   7 _____
4 _____   8 _____

B Match the photos with words from Exercise 1A.

LISTENING

2 A Look at the picture. What do you think the other man says?

B ▶ 3.1 Listen to the conversation. Are the sentences true (T) or false (F)?

1 Terry doesn't like the painting. _____
2 The painting is black and white. _____
3 David thinks you don't always have to understand art. _____
4 The painting was expensive. _____
5 Terry thinks he can paint it in five days. _____
6 Mary will be back in five minutes. _____

C Listen again. What are the answers to Terry's questions?

1 How much did the painting cost?

_____

2 Has Mary seen the painting?

_____

3 Does Mary like modern art?

_____

D Read audio script 3.1 on page 78 and find words that match these meanings.

1 very bad

_____

2 everywhere (2 words)

_____

3 an idea in a film, painting, etc. that someone is trying to tell people about

_____

4 a person who paints pictures

_____

5 not here

_____

6 something you don't expect

_____

GRAMMAR

QUESTIONS WITHOUT AUXILIARIES

3 A Complete the questions with the phrases in the box.

Who invented	Who earned	How many	Who uses
Which French	Which city	Who spends	
What country	Which painting	Which Caribbean	

1 _____ makes the most films every year?

2 _____ the World Wide Web?

3 _____ by van Gogh cost more: *Sunflowers* or *Portrait of Dr Gachet*?

4 _____ country invented the modern version of the dance called salsa?

5 _____ museum appears in the novel *The Da Vinci Code*?

6 _____ more time outdoors: people in New Zealand or people in Canada?

7 _____ people visit the Eiffel Tower every year?

8 _____ the internet more: Canadians or Americans?

9 _____ $1 million for each episode of *The Big Bang Theory* in 2014?

10 _____ has the most famous carnival every year?

B Match answers a)–j) with questions 1–10 in Exercise 3A.

a) the Louvre _____

b) Canadians _____

c) *Portrait of Dr Gachet* _____

d) Cuba _____

e) nearly seven million _____

f) Jim Parsons, for his role as Sheldon Cooper _____

g) Tim Berners-Lee _____

h) people in New Zealand _____

i) India _____

j) Rio de Janeiro _____

4 Write questions for the underlined answers. Start with *who*, *what*, *whose* or *how many*.

1 <u>Larry Page and Sergey Brin</u> started Google in the late 1990s.
   Who started Google in the late 1990s?

2 <u>Dr James Naismith</u> invented basketball in 1891.
   _____
   _____

3 Canadians spend <u>over forty hours</u> a month online.
   _____
   _____

4 <u>Charles Miller</u> brought football to Brazil from England in the nineteenth century.
   _____
   _____

5 <u>Jerry Seinfeld's</u> sitcom is one of the most successful TV shows of all time.
   _____
   _____

6 <u>Iepe Rubingh</u> first developed the sport of chess boxing in the 1990s.
   _____
   _____

7 <u>Germany</u> won the World Cup in 2014.
   _____
   _____

8 <u>The Carcross Desert</u> in Canada is the smallest desert in the world.
   _____
   _____

9 <u>Elvis Presley's</u> daughter is called Lisa Marie.
   _____
   _____

10 <u>Nearly seven million people</u> visit the British Museum every year.
   _____
   _____

VOCABULARY

COLLOCATIONS

1 A Find **seven verbs** in the puzzle.

A	R	R	A	N	G	E	V
C	A	N	C	E	L	M	O
H	B	Y	H	A	V	E	D
A	O	E	E	I	G	P	I
N	O	S	C	L	F	N	T
G	K	T	K	P	E	L	A
E	R	O	O	C	T	K	L
T	M	F	A	E	S	R	K

B There is a verb missing in each sentence. Complete the sentences with verbs from Exercise 1A.

arrange

1 Did you ⁄ to meet friends? If you didn't, we can meet later.
2 She called me because she wanted to a chat.
3 Please a table for us at the Blue Fin Restaurant tonight.
4 There's been a problem and I can't attend, so I'm calling to my reservation.
5 Don't forget to the train times before you leave for the station.
6 I'd like to come to the 4.30 performance, not the 6.30 one, and I'm calling to my ticket.
7 The manager of Triad Books is on the phone. He wants to business.

FUNCTION

MAKING A PHONE CALL

2 Match the sentence halves.

1 Who's
2 Hello, this
3 Can I speak
4 Can I
5 I'm afraid she's
6 I'll ask her
7 Thanks for

a) calling.
b) to call you back.
c) leave a message?
d) is John.
e) calling?
f) not here at the moment.
g) to Alexandra, please?

3 Find and correct four mistakes in the conversation.

A: Hello. I'm Jim. Is Trudy there?
B: I'm afraid but she's not here at the moment.
A: Oh really? Can I leave the message?
B: Of course.
A: Can you tell her that we need to discuss the party on Friday?
B: Yes, I will. I'll ask her for calling you back.
A: Thanks a lot.
B: You're welcome. Bye.
A: Bye.

4 Number the sentences in the correct order to make a phone conversation.

a) Yes. I'm going to be twenty minutes late. _____
b) Thank you very much. See you soon. _____
c) One moment. Who's calling please? _____
d) Hello. Can I speak to Kim? _____
e) Thanks for calling. Bye. _____
f) Good morning. Craven Beauty Parlour. Beverley speaking. _____
g) No problem. I'll tell her. _____
h) It's Liz Holder here. _____
i) Hi, Liz. Oh, I'm afraid Kim's at lunch. Is it about today's appointment? _____
j) Bye. ___10___

LEARN TO

MANAGE PHONE PROBLEMS

5 Put the words in the correct order to complete the questions.

1 **A:** Hi, I'm waiting for a delivery of fifteen chocolate rabbits. Have you sent them yet?
 B: One moment. _____?
 (name, / the / please / what's)
2 **A:** Hello, this is Hillary Kenton, calling from Newark.
 B: Sorry, _____. (catch / that / didn't / I) Did you say Hillary Clinton from New York?
3 **A:** Hello, my name is Aloysius Venoziak Menkovsky.
 B: _____? (repeat / you / can / that)
4 **A:** Hi, um … I'm … um … waiting for a … er … a package from Dublin.
 B: Sorry, _____?
 (speak / you / up, / can / please)
5 **A:** Hello. I'd like to order two Pentium Bidmark 6.40 large photocopiers, three Ribdale Energy Star fax machines, five Rubicon Jump Drives, and …
 B: Sorry, _____?
 (down, / slow / you / can / please)

LISTENING

6 ▶ 3.2 Listen to three phone conversations and complete the notes.

1 Pauline calling. No _____ for the concert. Call back tonight _____

2 Elise called. Meet her at the _____ at _____

3 Roundhouse Bar and Grill doesn't take _____ Come before _____

GRAMMAR QUESTION FORMS

1 A Complete the questions with a question word or an auxiliary verb.

1 When _____*does*_____ the film start?
2 _____ often do you see your grandmother?
3 _____ are my keys? I can't find them.
4 _____ you enjoy watching films?
5 _____ you know Sabina? She's my best friend.
6 _____ do you usually go on holiday?
7 _____ many hours do you work?
8 _____ time did you get here? I'm sorry I'm late.

B Match answers a)–h) with questions 1–8 in Exercise 1A.

a) About five minutes ago. Don't worry, it's no problem. _____
b) No, I don't. Hi, Sabina. _____
c) Once or twice a year. _____
d) We usually go to Spain. My aunt has a house there. _____
e) Here they are. They were on the television! _____
f) Yes, I do. But I don't like horror films. _____
g) Usually about thirty-five hours a week. _____
h) In half an hour. _____

VOCABULARY PHRASES WITH *GET, GO, HAVE, SPEND*

2 A Write the words in the box in the correct column.

| married children money on clothes a barbecue time off work the bus time with family on well on holiday to the cinema sightseeing |

get	go	have	spend
married			

B Which phrases from Exercise 2A would you use for situations 1–7?

1 You meet someone you like and want to spend your life together. _____*get married*_____
2 You travel home on public transport.
_____
3 You visit your mother every day.
_____
4 You do this to watch a film.
_____
5 You eat in the garden and the food is cooked over a fire. _____
6 You have a good relationship with someone.
_____
7 You visit the places tourists see in a city.
_____

GRAMMAR PAST SIMPLE

3 Complete the article with the past simple form of the verbs in brackets.

ANGRY MOTHER PUNISHES SIXTY-ONE-YEAR-OLD SON

An angry mother [1] _____ (take) the house keys and money away from her sixty-one-year-old son because he [2] _____ (stay) out late at night and [3] _____ (not tell) her where he planned to go when he [4] _____ (go out). The mother, who is eighty-one years old, even went to the police in Caltagione, Italy, the town where she lives. She [5] _____ (ask) the police to tell her son that he should 'grow up' and behave in a better way towards his mother.

The son [6] _____ (complain) that it was his mother who [7] _____ (be) the problem. 'It's not my fault,' he [8] _____ (tell) reporters. 'She always treats me badly. And her cooking is really awful!'

A policeman [9] _____ (talk) to the mother and the son, and they finally [10] _____ (decide) to go home together.

FUNCTION MAKING CONVERSATION

4 A Complete the words in the conversations.

1 **A:** Hello. My name's Felipe. It's n_*ice*_ to meet you.
   B: Hi, I'm Magda. Nice to meet you, t_ _ _.
2 **A:** Nice day, i_ _ 't it?
   B: Yes, it's l_v_ly.
3 **A:** S_, where exactly do you c_m_ from?
   B: Zaragoza. It's a small c_ty in Northern Spain.
4 **A:** Did you have a g_ _d w_ _k_ _d?
   B: Yes, it was OK. I didn't d_ m_ch.
5 **A:** So, w_ _ _ _d you l_k_ a dr_ _k?
   B: Yes, I'd l_v_ a glass of w_t_r.
6 **A:** I'll s_ _ you l_t_r.
   B: S_ _ you s_ _ n.

B ▶ R1.1 Listen and check.

GRAMMAR PRESENT SIMPLE AND CONTINUOUS

5 Find and correct the mistakes in the sentences.

don't like
1 I ⟨am not liking fish.
2 I stay with some friends for a few days so I can look for somewhere to live.
3 I'm not knowing what time the lesson starts.
4 They spend time with their family in Germany at the moment.
5 We're usually going out for a pizza about once a week.
6 I'm not understanding where Ian is. He never arrives late.
7 Do you watch this programme, or can I watch the football on the other channel?

GRAMMAR ADVERBS OF FREQUENCY

6 The words in bold are in the wrong place in the sentences. Correct the sentences.

1 We come (always) here. It's the best club in the area.
2 **Hardly ever** I see her because she works for a different company.
3 My **occasionally** parents help us when we're busy.
4 I get up at **usually** about 6.30a.m.
5 Sal's very upset – she wants to see him **never** again.
6 We go to **once in a while** Scotland.
7 **Rarely** I have the chance to spend time with my sister.
8 I take the children **every day** to school.

FUNCTION LIKES/DISLIKES

7 Complete the second sentence so that it has the same meaning as the first sentence. Use the words in brackets.

1 I don't enjoy getting up early. (not very keen)
 I ____'m not very keen on____ getting up early.
2 I like punk music very much. (absolutely)
 I _____ punk music.
3 I hate sales reps who try to sell me products on the telephone (stand)
 I _____ sales reps who try to sell me products on the telephone.
4 Marjorie isn't very keen on doing housework. (like)
 Marjorie _____ doing housework.
5 I'm quite happy to do physical jobs. (mind)
 I _____ doing physical jobs.
6 John really doesn't like eating spicy food. (hate)
 John _____ eating spicy food.
7 I'm happy working in a team. (like)
 I _____ in a team.
8 I enjoy walking in the countryside. (keen)
 I _____ walking in the countryside.

GRAMMAR PRESENT CONTINUOUS/BE GOING TO FOR FUTURE

8 Underline the correct alternatives.

1 *I'm going/I going to go* shopping later. Do you want to come?
2 My sister *is/is going to* having a party on Friday, but I don't know what to wear.
3 He *starting/'s going to start* karate lessons in January.
4 So, *are you/are you going to* staying with your parents for the weekend?
5 I'm not *coming/going to coming* to the lesson this evening.
6 *We're/We're going to* flying to Italy on 19 December.

VOCABULARY WORK; TIME OUT

9 Complete the words in the sentences.

1 Pete gets a good s__l__ry, but he doesn't like his b__ss.
2 I love going s__ghts__ __ __ng when I'm on holiday.
3 We w__rk under a lot of pr__ss__re in the busy months.
4 There were some wonderful photographs in the exh__b__t__ __n.
5 The best thing about the job is that I g__t very l__ng h__l__d__ys.
6 We bought this painting from that new __rt g__ll__r__ in West Street.
7 I love their music and I really wanted to go to their c__nc__rt, but I didn't have enough money for the t__ck__t.
8 I enjoy my job because I can always find an interesting t__sk to do.

GRAMMAR QUESTIONS WITH/WITHOUT AUXILIARIES

10 A The auxiliary verb is missing in eight of the questions. Add the missing auxiliary where necessary.

       is
1 Who / your teacher?
2 Where you come from?
3 Who forgot to bring the keys?
4 Why David leave his job?
5 How often you play football?
6 How much it cost to fly to Russia?
7 Which class won the competition?
8 Who wrote *The Jungle Book*?
9 When you last go to a concert?
10 Whose bag is that?
11 Why you learning English?
12 Where you buy that coat?

B Match answers a)–l) with questions 1–12 in Exercise 10A.

a) Our class did. We won the competition! _____
b) About €300. _____
c) It's mine. Sorry, I left it there. _____
d) I come from Argentina. _____
e) I want to study in the USA. _____
f) Zavier. He always forgets things. _____
g) I play once or twice a week. _____
h) He didn't like his boss. _____
i) Two months ago. I saw a really good jazz trio. _____
j) Rudyard Kipling. _____
k) I bought it in Toronto last year. _____
l) Her name's Mrs Taylor. _____

CHECK

Circle the correct option to complete the sentences.

1 What _____ the time?
   a) be   **b)** 's   **c)** are

2 When _____ start work?
   a) do you   **b)** are you   **c)** you do

3 They _____ married in 2013.
   a) get   **b)** are getting   **c)** got

4 I _____ €100 on these boots and they're broken.
   a) spend   **b)** spent   **c)** paid

5 Why _____ you sad? Is there a problem?
   a) do   **b)** is   **c)** are

6 We _____ in love the first time we saw each other.
   a) fell   **b)** felt   **c)** fall

7 When _____ to the UK?
   a) moved you   **b)** did you move   **c)** did you moved

8 She _____ and walked away.
   a) smile   **b)** smiled   **c)** smiles

9 When I _____ college, I started looking for a job.
   a) leave   **b)** am leaving   **c)** left

10 Did you _____ a good weekend?
   a) have   **b)** get   **c)** like

11 Where _____ do you come from?
   a) absolutely   **b)** really   **c)** exactly

12 I usually _____ to Helen when I have a problem.
   a) am talking   **b)** talk   **c)** talked

13 We like to keep our prices low. This makes our _____ happy.
   a) customers   **b)** employee   **c)** staff

14 I'm looking for a job with a higher _____.
   a) boss   **b)** salary   **c)** task

15 At the moment I _____ a book about a young boy in Afghanistan.
   a) 'm reading   **b)** read   **c)** going to read

16 I can't _____ computer games. I really hate them.
   a) hate   **b)** stand   **c)** keen

17 It's important to _____ good relationships with the other employees.
   a) get   **b)** make   **c)** have

18 I look forward to _____ from you.
   a) hearing   **b)** heard   **c)** hear

19 It's a dangerous job: you _____ your life every day.
   a) work   **b)** deal with   **c)** risk

20 We _____ a lot of different problems.
   a) work   **b)** deal with   **c)** risk

21 I'm not very keen _____ violent films.
   a) of   **b)** about   **c)** on

22 Eve _____ to Australia next month.
   a) is going   **b)** went   **c)** go

23 I _____ dinner tonight. I'm just going to have a snack.
   a) don't have   **b)** 'm not having   **c)** don't having

24 _____ to come out on Saturday night?
   a) Do you like   **b)** Would you like   **c)** Are you liking

25 I'm afraid Ella isn't here at the moment. Can I _____ a message?
   a) make   **b)** give   **c)** take

26 I bought these souvenirs at a _____ market in Greece.
   a) street   **b)** shopping   **c)** nature

27 We can't go to the restaurant, so we'll have to _____ our reservation.
   a) arrange   **b)** book   **c)** cancel

28 Hello. Petra _____. Can I help you?
   a) is speaking   **b)** speaking   **c)** I'm speaking

29 Hi, Mike. Pleased _____ you. I'm Nia.
   a) of meeting   **b)** I met   **c)** to meet

30 What are your plans for the weekend? _____ anything nice?
   a) Are you doing   **b)** Did you do   **c)** Do you do

RESULT   /30

VOCABULARY:
MAKE AND DO

1 A Complete the phrases with *make* or *do*.

1 _____ a speech
2 _____ well/badly
3 _____ a project
4 _____ a phone call
5 _____ business
6 _____ a decision
7 _____ my homework
8 _____ a meal

B Write answers beginning with *I made* or *I did*. Use the words in brackets.

1 How did you lose weight? (decision)
I made a decision to start eating healthily.

2 How did you contact her? (phone)
_____

3 How do you know Ben Garmin? (business)
_____

4 I heard the restaurant was closed, so what did you do? (meal)
_____

5 What type of work did you do at school today? (project)
_____

6 What did you do in the library after school? (homework)
_____

7 How did the Public Speaking conference finish? (speech)
_____

8 How was the singing competition? (well)
_____

GRAMMAR:
PRESENT PERFECT + *EVER/NEVER*

2 Complete the sentences with the present perfect form of the verbs in brackets.

1 I _____*'ve never been*_____ (never / be) on TV.
2 _____ (you / ever / sing) to an audience?
3 Sheena and Rick _____ (never / travel) by train.
4 My granddad _____ (never / use) a computer.
5 _____ (she / ever / make) a speech?
6 _____ (you / ever / lie) to your best friend?
8 Lisa _____ (never / eat) octopus.
7 _____ (you / ever / win) a competition?

3 Circle the correct sentence in each pair.

1 **a)** I've first played the guitar when I was a teenager.
   b) I first played the guitar when I was a teenager.

2 **a)** When you worked in Hollywood, have you ever met anyone famous?
   b) When you worked in Hollywood, did you ever meet anyone famous?

3 **a)** Have you ever eaten sushi? Try some!
   b) Did you ever eat sushi? Try some!

4 **a)** Last night I read until 2a.m.
   b) Last night I've read until 2a.m.

5 **a)** Did you ever see the film *No Country for Old Men*? I have the DVD.
   b) Have you ever seen the film *No Country for Old Men*? I have the DVD.

6 **a)** In 1989 the government did something that changed the world.
   b) In 1989 the government has done something that changed the world.

7 **a)** She has never been to the theatre.
   b) She has ever been to the theatre.

8 **a)** I've ever worked in retail in my life.
   b) I've never worked in retail in my life.

4 Underline the correct alternatives.

Hi Janine,

I ¹*was/'ve* been here for a week now and already I ²*made/'ve made* lots of friends. I share a room with a man called Don. Yesterday he asked me, ³'*Did you ever spend/Have you ever spent* time in a place like this?' I told him, 'I ⁴*went/have been* camping when I was ten.' He ⁵*laughed/has laughed*! He ⁶*spent/has spent* half his life here!

There are lots of things to do: there's a gym, a cinema, a library and a few clubs. I ⁷*didn't have/haven't had* time to join any clubs yet, but this afternoon we ⁸*watched/have watched* a film in the cinema.

The only bad thing is the food. I ⁹*didn't ever eat/'ve never eaten* such terrible food before in my whole life!

Best wishes,

Bob

MORE THAN A HOBBY

Gordon Ramsay   Winston Churchill   Woody Allen

1 When Wallace Stevens walked into his office every morning, his colleagues didn't know about his secret: Stevens lived a double life. By day he worked for an insurance company. The rest of his life was spent becoming one of the greatest American poets of the twentieth century.

2 Secret talent is more common than we think, even with people who are already famous in one area. Take Luciano Pavarotti, who was one of the world's greatest classical singers. Not many people know that before he became a singer, he was an outstanding football player. The same is true of TV chef Gordon Ramsay, who is now well-known for his brilliant cooking and his bad language. Ramsay played professional football for Glasgow Rangers, one of Scotland's best teams.

3 A number of politicians first made their name in other jobs. Most people know that Arnold Schwarzenegger had a very successful acting career before becoming Governor of California. Winston Churchill, prime minister of Great Britain, also had another talent: he wrote great history books. Churchill's books won him the Nobel Prize in Literature in 1953. Václav Havel, who was the first president of the Czech Republic, was also a great writer.

4 There are also musicians and actors who have secret talents. Paul McCartney and David Bowie are both painters, Paul Newman was a racing car driver and actor Colin Farrell is a professional line dancer. And only those who go to a little hotel bar in New York City every Monday would know that one of the best clarinet players in town is actor and film director Woody Allen. He certainly plays the clarinet better than Bill Clinton plays the saxophone!

READING

5 A Do you recognise any of the people in the photos? Why are they famous? What else are/were they good at? Read the article to find out.

B Read the article again. Are the sentences true (T) or false (F)?

1 The people in the text are famous for one thing, but also good at another thing. _____
2 Wallace Stevens' colleagues didn't know he was a poet. _____
3 Gordon Ramsay was a chef before he became a famous footballer. _____
4 Churchill and Havel were both actors and politicians. _____
5 Woody Allen plays the clarinet and the saxophone. _____

C Circle the correct meaning for the words and phrases from the text.

1 lived a double life (paragraph 1)
   a) had two very different lifestyles
   b) had a difficult life
2 the same is true of (paragraph 2)
   a) this situation is very different from
   b) this situation is very similar to
3 bad language (paragraph 2)
   a) speaking badly about another person
   b) saying bad words
4 made their name (paragraph 3)
   a) became famous
   b) learnt to do something

WRITING

CORRECTING MISTAKES

6 Find and correct nine mistakes in the text: three grammar (gr), three spelling (sp) and three punctuation (p).

THE GREATEST MIND IN FICTION

belong (gr)

Most of fiction's great minds ~~belongs~~ ʌ either to criminals or to the men and women who catch them. A greatest of these is probably Sherlock Holmes. The Holmes stories were written by Sir Arthur Conan Doyle a docter from edinburgh, Scotland. Conan Doyle knew a lot about the human body and pollice work, and he has used this information in his books. Very quickly, Conan Doyle's hero beccame popular. When Holmes was killed in one story, thousands of readers protested. Conan Doyle changed his mind, and Holmes appeared in another story

VOCABULARY
EDUCATION

1 Read the clues and complete the crossword.

```
M A K E
```

Across

1 One of the best things about going to university is that you _____make_____ a lot of new friends.

4 On Friday, we have to do a _____, so I need to learn the vocabulary.

7 I'd love to play the _____, but our flat is too small to have one – so I play the guitar instead!

8 At my school we play a lot of _____. It keeps us fit.

10 I don't study _____ very often because I don't have internet access at home.

11 I have to _____ an exam at the end of the year.

Down

1 I don't like speaking French because I make a lot of _____.

2 At the end of the year all the students give a _____.

3 When you _____ art, you learn about painters like Picasso and Salvador Dalí.

5 I'd like to study foreign _____ like Russian and Spanish.

6 At school we didn't have to wear a _____. We wore our own clothes.

9 Every week we _____ games like tennis or netball.

GRAMMAR
CAN, HAVE TO, MUST

2 Read the advertisements and complete the conversations with *can, can't, have to* or *don't have to*.

LEARN TO PLAY MUSIC – BEGINNERS' CLASS
Always wanted to play the drums? Or the guitar? Want to try the piano? Come and join us for fun music lessons. Try any instrument you want, and we'll help you learn to play. No previous experience necessary. We supply the instruments, so you don't need to bring your own. Children and adults welcome.

Conversation 1

Susan: Hi. I'd like to come to the beginners' music class. Do I [1] _____have to_____ be able to play an instrument?

Teacher: No, you [2] _____ play an instrument. You [3] _____ choose your instrument here, and we'll help you to learn.

Susan: [4] _____ I come to a lesson first to see if I like it?

Teacher: Well, I'm afraid you [5] _____ come to the lessons unless you sign up for the whole course.

Susan: OK. [6] _____ I bring children?

Teacher: Yes, you [7] _____. Children love it.

Susan: Do I [8] _____ bring my own instrument?

Teacher: No, we have instruments here you [9] _____ use.

Join our Arabic language and culture course
Full price: £180   Reduced rates for students: £130

Just come along to the first class. No need to register first, just bring an enrolment form with you. Pay after the class if you wish to enrol.

Conversation 2

Student: I'm a student. How much do I [1] _____ pay?

Secretary: It's a reduced rate, so you only [2] _____ pay £130.

Student: Do I [3] _____ register first?

Secretary: No, you [4] _____ to register. You [5] _____ come along to the first class. If you like the class, you [6] _____ complete the form at the end of the lesson.

Student: [7] _____ I pay by cheque?

Secretary: Yes, you [8] _____ pay by card or cheque on the night.

3 A ▶ 4.1 Listen and complete the sentences.

1 How much _____ pay?
2 _____ park here?
3 _____ visit her before we leave.
4 _____ stay in this hotel.
5 _____ wear that!
6 _____ tell anyone.

B Practise saying the sentences.

4 A Rewrite the sentences. Replace the underlined words with phrases with *can/can't*.

1 You <u>are not allowed to</u> have your mobile phone switched on.

2 You have to register before <u>it's possible to</u> use the site.

3 I'm afraid <u>it isn't possible for her to</u> speak to you at the moment.

4 <u>It's OK to</u> use my computer if you want to.

B Rewrite the sentences. Replace the underlined words with phrases with *have to/don't have to* or *must/mustn't*. There may be more than one possible answer.

1 <u>It's necessary to</u> be good at foreign languages if you want to learn Mandarin.

2 <u>It's important to</u> be there on time or they won't let us in.

3 <u>It isn't necessary for us to</u> have a licence to fish here.

4 <u>It's important that you don't</u> tell him I'm here.

5 Look at the exam rules and complete the conversation with *can/can't*, *have to/don't have to* or *must/mustn't*. There may be more than one possible answer.

EXAM RULES

mobile phones	✗
talk to other students	✗
arrive on time	✓
eat/drink in the examination room	✗ (but water OK)
have a dictionary	✓

Teacher: Are there any questions?

Dan: Yes. ¹_____*Can*_____ we bring our mobile phones into the room?

Teacher: No, you ²_____. You ³_____ turn them off and leave them outside in your bag.

Julie: Is it OK to eat during the exam?

Teacher: No. You ⁴_____ have a bottle of water, but you ⁵_____ have anything else to eat or drink.

Marco: Do we ⁶_____ leave our dictionaries in our bags?

Teacher: No, you ⁷_____ bring dictionaries into the examination.

Dan: What happens if we arrive late?

Teacher: You ⁸_____ arrive on time or you ⁹_____ come into the examination room.

Julie: ¹⁰_____ we talk to other students?

Teacher: No. You ¹¹_____ talk at all during the examination. Now, does everybody understand? Is everything clear?

LISTENING

6 A ▶ 4.2 Listen to the first part of an interview about different types of learner. Match the pictures with the types of learner.

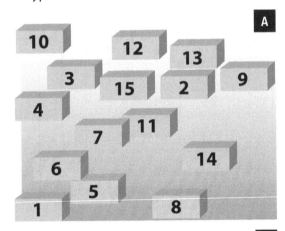

1 Picture _____: holist – learns lots of information about a topic, but in no particular order

2 Picture _____: serialist – learns things in sequence from the bottom up

B ▶ 4.3 Listen to the second part of the interview. Are the sentences about serialists (S) or holists (H)?

1 This learner likes to understand detail. _____

2 This learner reads instructions before using a new piece of equipment. _____

3 This learner might read a chapter from the middle of a book first. _____

4 This learner makes a careful plan before writing. _____

5 This learner reads around the topic and makes lots of notes before writing. _____

C Circle the correct option to complete the statements.

1 Students
   a) are always either serialists or holists.
   b) often use both serialist and holist approaches.

2 Serialists like to learn things
   a) in the correct order.
   b) in any order.

3 A holist likes to have an idea of the 'big picture' and
   a) doesn't worry about detail.
   b) thinks that the detail is very important.

VOCABULARY

LANGUAGE LEARNING

1 Complete the words in the sentences.

1 I find remembering new words very difficult, so I try to m_ _ _ _ise five to ten words a day. I write each word in a sentence and then say the sentence again and again in my head.

2 If I don't understand the meaning of a word, I l_ _k it u_ in a dictionary.

3 Sometimes I rer_ _d an article for a second time, looking for new words and phrases.

4 I like to ch_ _ on the internet. I speak to other learners from all over the world.

5 I like watching films in English, especially ones with su_ _ _ _ _s.

6 It's a good idea to g_ on_ _ _ _ to read websites in English.

7 I always n_ _ _ _ d_ _ _ any new words or phrases in my vocabulary notebook, then look back at them later and try to use them.

FUNCTION

GIVING ADVICE

2 Read the questions asking for advice. Put the words in the correct order to complete the answers.

> I'm thinking about changing my hairstyle. Any ideas?

1 _____ (think / don't / you / I / should) change it. It looks great.

2 _____ (try / why / you / don't) red and black stripes? It's cool.

> I don't know what to buy my husband for his birthday. His only interest is watching sport.

3 _____ (should / think / I / get / you) him a pair of trainers and tell him to do some sport instead of watching it all day!

4 _____ (you / don't / why / buy) him some tickets to a football match?

> I'm going to babysit for my nephew (3) and niece (6). I've never done this before. Can anyone help?

5 _____ (try / think / I / should / you) to make a simple recipe, like chocolate biscuits or a cake. They'll enjoy helping you.

6 _____ (idea / it's / think / a / to / good) about the things you enjoyed doing as a child: colouring, making things, singing songs, etc.

3 Read the problems and complete the advice using the words in brackets.

> I'm 29 years old and I work in a bank. I love my job, I have good friends and a boyfriend who loves me. I don't understand why I'm not happy. I'm always so stressed. Why can't I just be happy?

1 _____ (think / should) sit down and work out what is making you feel unhappy.

2 _____ (why not) write a list of the things that you are happy about in your life, and a list of the things that are not right?

3 _____ (try / talk) about your problems with your boyfriend. Does he understand?

> I have my end of university exams next month. I'm so frightened that I'm not going to pass them that I'm thinking of leaving university, and not going to the exams. I've studied hard but now I feel like I don't know anything.

4 _____ (not think / good idea) leave the university. If you've studied hard, you probably have nothing to worry about.

5 _____ (why / you / try) talking to your university professor? He/She can probably help.

6 _____ (think / should) try some relaxation techniques to help you with the exam stress.

LEARN TO

RESPOND TO ADVICE

4 A Match advice 1–6 with responses a)–f). Then complete the responses.

1 Why don't we go to the cinema tonight?
2 I don't think you should buy that car.
3 I think we should organise a party.
4 Maybe you should say sorry.
5 You shouldn't play so many computer games.
6 I think you should study more.

a) I _____ so. I'll call Louise later.
b) _____ right. I need to get out more.
c) That's _____ idea. Do you know what's on?
d) I suppose _____ . I want to do well in the exam.
e) I'm not _____ a good idea. We're too busy.
f) You're _____ . It's too expensive.

B ▶ 4.4 Listen and check.

C ▶ 4.5 Listen to the advice again. Say the responses.

5 TRAVEL

VOCABULARY

TRANSPORT

1 A Find fourteen types of transport in the word snake.

taxi shipmotorbiketrammmopedaeroplanelorryspeedboathelicoptercoachferryhotairballoonundergroundminibus

B Complete the word web with the types of transport in Exercise 1A.

WATER
8 _____
9 _____
10 _____

FOUR WHEELS OR MORE
1 taxi
2 _____
3 _____
4 _____

TWO WHEELS
11 _____
12 _____

TRANSPORT

AIR
5 _____
6 _____
7 _____

PUBLIC TRANSPORT (CITY)
13 _____
14 _____

C What types of transport are the people talking about?

1 'I always call one to get home at night.'
   taxi

2 'I use it every morning to get to work. The roads are full of cars, so it's the quickest way to travel.'
   _____

3 'It's my dream to travel in one of these, to feel the wind in my face and look down at the world below.' _____

4 'We enjoy touring foreign cities in them. They are perfect for groups of thirty or forty people.'
   _____

5 'I drive it for twelve hours a day. It's my job. I transport products for food companies across the country.' _____

6 'I can take you to your house. It's big enough for two people and I have two helmets.' _____

7 'It's the fastest way to travel on water. I use mine for waterskiing.' _____

8 'In the past, everyone used these to visit other continents. It took three weeks to get to the USA! Now this type of travel is only for rich people.'
   _____

GRAMMAR

PAST SIMPLE AND PAST CONTINUOUS

2 Match the sentence halves.

1 The last time they spoke to Marina _____
2 The teacher explained the exercise to us, but _____
3 Were there any calls for me _____
4 It started to rain _____
5 My mobile phone rang while _____
6 I fell asleep while I _____
7 Were you doing something important _____
8 I didn't go out last night _____

a) while we were playing football.
b) when I phoned you?
c) while I was shopping?
d) I was cooking.
e) because I was studying.
f) we weren't listening.
g) she was working in a bar.
h) was watching TV.

3 Complete the conversations with the past simple or past continuous form of the verbs in brackets.

Conversation 1

A: I came to see you yesterday, but you weren't at home. What [1] _were you doing_ (you/do)?

B: I was here, but I [2] _____ (play) with my son in the garden, so I [3] _____ (not hear) the doorbell.

Conversation 2

A: I heard you broke your leg. How [4] _____ (it/happen)?

B: It happened when I [5] _____ (climb) a mountain two weeks ago. I fell and I [6] _____ (land) badly.

Conversation 3

A: Wendy told me you [7] _____ (see) Jim last week.

B: Yes. I [8] _____ (study) in the library and he [9] _____ (say) 'hello'.

Conversation 4

A: I hear you crashed the car again. [10] _____ (you/drive) too fast?

B: No! It wasn't my fault! I [11] _____ (go) at thirty miles an hour when this other car suddenly [12] _____ (come) out of a side street.

Conversation 5

A: I [13] _____ (see) you on your bicycle yesterday. Where [14] _____ (you/go)?

B: I [15] _____ (go) to the shops, but I [16] _____ (drop) my wallet on the way!

4 A Match the phrases in the box with the pictures.

> drop his ticket   try to sleep
> decide to use his mobile phone   go for a walk
> go through security   pay the taxi driver

B Complete the story with the past simple or past continuous form of the phrases in Exercise 4A.

This is the story of Tim Bobo's first trip in an aeroplane. He was very excited, but as he was going out of the house, he ¹ _dropped his ticket_ on the floor. He took a taxi to the airport, but while he ² _____, someone took his bag. Luckily, there was nothing important in the bag. He checked in, but while he ³ _____, he found some keys in his pocket. Soon he was on the aeroplane. When it was taking off, he ⁴ _____ around the plane! The flight attendant told him to sit down immediately. Then soon after this he noticed that everyone seemed unhappy, so he started singing. Unfortunately, the other passengers ⁵ _____ and they told him to be quiet. A few hours later, he made one more mistake: while the plane was landing, he ⁶ _____ his mobile phone!

5 A ▶ 5.1 Listen to the pronunciation of *was* and *were* in the sentences. Then listen again and repeat.

B Read audio script 5.1 on page 79. Listen again, read and repeat.

LISTENING

6 A ▶ 5.2 Listen to a story about a German tourist. Choose the map which shows his journey.

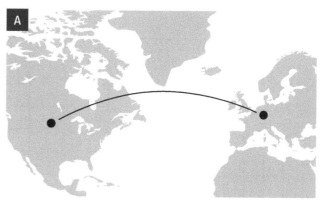

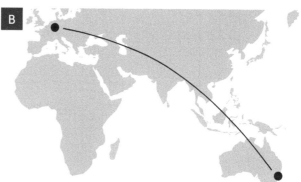

B Listen again. Are the sentences true (T) or false (F)?

1 A German man wanted to visit his girlfriend in Sydney, Australia. _____
2 When he was booking his ticket, he made a mistake. _____
3 His flight took him to the wrong town in Australia. _____
4 He was wearing summer clothes because the weather in Montana was hot. _____
5 His parents and friends sent him warm clothes. _____
6 After a few days, he bought a ticket to Australia. _____

7 A Read the sentences from the recording. Can you remember the rest of the second sentence?

1 A twenty-one-year-old German tourist called Tobi Gutt wanted to visit his girlfriend in Sydney, Australia. Unfortunately, _____ _____ .
2 When he looked at the plane to Sidney, he became confused. Strangely, _____ _____ .
3 A few friendly people helped him with food and drink until eventually, _____ _____ .

B ▶ 5.3 Listen, check and complete the sentences.

VOCABULARY
TRAVEL ITEMS

1 A Read the clues and complete the crossword.

Across

3 You use this to take photos and put them on your computer.

7 You write names, addresses and ideas in this.

8 You put this on your head when the sun is very hot.

9 You pack your clothes in this. It is hard and sometimes has wheels.

Down

1 You wear these when it rains.

2 You wear these on your feet when you climb a mountain or go for a long walk.

4 You buy these to remember the places you visited.

5 You use these to look at birds and animals that are far away.

6 You carry important documents and money in this so they are safe.

B Complete the sentences with the words in Exercise 1A.

1 I wrote her phone number in my _notebook_ .

2 Before we leave for the airport, I'd like to buy some _____ for my friends.

3 It's very hot. You'll need to wear a _____ _____.

4 These _____ _____ are new and my feet are really hurting.

5 It's raining. We'll have to wear some _____ _____.

6 Can you see that beautiful bird? Have a look through the _____.

7 My passport was in my _____ _____, but I took it off when I went swimming.

8 Thirty kilos. I'm afraid your _____ is too heavy. You'll need to pay extra.

9 I wanted to take some photos, but I left my _____ _____ at home.

GRAMMAR
VERB PATTERNS

2 Underline the correct alternatives.

1 I really enjoy *to read/reading* in bed before I go to sleep.

2 My brother wants *to see/seeing* you before he leaves.

3 We chose *to get/getting* married in Venice because that's where we first met.

4 My parents love *spend/spending* time with their grandchildren.

5 It always seems *to rain/raining* when I come to stay.

6 The company decided *to refund/refunding* the money we paid for the tickets.

7 We should avoid *to travel/travelling* when there is too much traffic.

8 The builders need *to finish/finishing* their work before we can paint the house.

9 We hope *to see/seeing* you again soon.

10 I must finish *to write/writing* this letter.

11 Just imagine *to live/living* in a place as beautiful as this!

12 I hate *to go/going* to the supermarket.

3 Write sentences using the prompts.

1 the children / love / play / on beach / in sun

The children love playing on the beach in the sun.

2 I / expect / hear from / travel agent / later today

_____

3 we / want / go / on holiday / but / we / too busy

_____

4 we / seem / go back / same place / every year

_____

5 Alan / chose / stay / in hotel

_____

6 we / enjoy / walk / and look at / beautiful countryside

_____

7 I / decided / travel / on my own

_____

8 we / avoid / visit / tourist resorts / in summer

_____

9 we / need / book / our flights / before / prices / go up

_____

READING

4 A Read the article and match topics a)–d) with paragraphs 1–4.

a) dealing with problems _____

b) having the best experience _____

c) doing something different _____

d) preparing for your trip _____

My top travel tips

Sandy Graves is an experienced travel writer who regularly travels all over the world. Here she shares some of her top tips.

1 When you start packing, leave your suitcase open somewhere. As you think of something you need to take, pack it. Don't leave it until later or you might forget. Make photocopies of all your important documents and put them in your suitcase, too. If you lose your passport, having a copy will make it easier to get a new one. Pack earplugs. They're great for long flights and noisy hostels, when you really need to sleep.

2 While you're travelling, be patient. Everybody wants to leave on time, but it doesn't always happen. Buses can be late, you can have problems with your documents or your card might not work in the ATM. Don't worry, there's always a way to get there. Smile and enjoy it – you won't have another chance to!

3 If you want more than just a holiday, try volunteering, spending some time learning new skills and meeting new people. You can travel anywhere in the world to do all kinds of different jobs, from building in Tanzania to looking after elephants in Thailand. Just think what you could do.

4 Do your best to try everything around you. Try the local food, buy the terrible, cheap souvenirs (they won't feel terrible when you're back home) and take lots of photos. And talk to local people – you can get so much more out of your trip if you do. Keep an open mind, and don't criticise the local culture. You might see or experience things which seem strange to you, but are normal there.

B Read the article again. Are the statements true (T) or false (F)?

1 Try to pack things at the same time as you think of them. _____

2 It's a good idea to take earplugs for when you want to go swimming. _____

3 It's best not to worry when you have problems. _____

4 There aren't many opportunities to do anything different when you travel. _____

5 Don't buy souvenirs if they're not good. _____

6 Try to accept things which seem strange to you. _____

C Find words in the article that match these meanings.

1 things you put in your ears to keep out noise (paragraph 1): _____

2 places where you can eat and sleep cheaply for a short time (paragraph 1): _____

3 able to wait calmly (paragraph 2): _____

4 a machine where you can get money from your bank (paragraph 2): _____

5 abilities; things you can do (paragraph 3): _____

6 from the place where you are (paragraph 4): _____

WRITING

USING SEQUENCERS

5 A Look at the pictures of two stories. Put sentences a)–i) in the correct order to tell the stories.

a) We had a great night out.

b) First, we met in a bar in town.

c) Finally, when we arrived, the hotel didn't have our reservation.

d) After the meal, we went dancing.

e) Then, our taxi broke down on the way to the hotel.

f) First, the flight was cancelled.

g) The holiday was a disaster.

h) Then we went out for a pizza.

i) We waited, and after a while we had to fly to a different airport.

Story 1

__*a*__ , _____ , _____ , _____

Story 2

__*g*__ , _____ , _____ , _____ , _____

B Write about a time when you went on holiday or had a good night out. Write 50–100 words. Use the sequencers in the box.

first   then   after that/after a while   finally

VOCABULARY

TOURISM

1 Match the sentence halves.

1 There were a lot of _____
2 I always wanted to be a tour _____
3 We went on a guided _____
4 They saw a lot of tourist attractions, including _____
5 I really enjoyed the boat trip _____
6 The best thing about Corsica is the scenery, which _____
7 Our boat took us under a _____

a) the History Museum and the National Art Gallery.
b) guide because I love showing people my city.
c) tour around the churches of Rome.
d) includes mountains, beaches and forests.
e) waterfall, which was fifty metres high.
f) down the River Nile.
g) tourists in our hotel.

FUNCTION

ASKING FOR/GIVING DIRECTIONS

2 Underline the correct alternatives. Where no word is necessary, choose (-).

1 For the police station, go straight *in/over/on* and you can't miss it.
2 Go *(-)/for/along* the main road until you see the sports field.
3 To reach the train station, you need to go *up/through/in* the centre of town.
4 Keep going *(-)/on/by* until you reach the corner of King's Road.
5 You'll find the bar *up/at/of* the corner.
6 Walk for two minutes and you'll see the school in front *of/by/to* you.
7 Take *to/(-)/on* the second left after the library and you'll see my house.
8 For the post office, go *past/through/on* the turning for the station.

3 A ▶ 5.4 Look at the map and listen to the directions. Where is the man trying to go?

1 *restaurant*
2 _____
3 _____
4 _____
5 _____
6 _____

B Read audio script 5.4 on page 79 to check your answers.

LEARN TO

SHOW/CHECK UNDERSTANDING

4 A Put the words in the correct order to complete the conversations.

Conversation 1
A: Excuse me. [1] _____ ?
(help / you / me / can) I'm looking for the Science Museum.
B: Go straight on. [2] _____ .
(can't / you / it / miss)

A: OK, so it's easy! [3] _____ ?
(map / you / the / me / on / can / show)
B: Yes, of course.

Conversation 2
A: Excuse me. I'm trying to find the internet café.
[4] _____ ? (the / this / way / right / is)
B: Yes. Keep going. [5] _____ .
(it / see / of / front / in / you / you'll)

A: [6] _____ ? (walk / I / can)
B: Yes, you can. [7] _____ .
(about / minutes / it / ten / takes)

Conversation 3
A: [8] _____ to the tube? (far / it / is)
B: No. It's about two minutes' walk.

A: OK. [9] _____ ?
(to / need / left / so / the / go / at / I / cinema)
B: That's right. It's easy!

B ▶ 5.5 Listen and check.

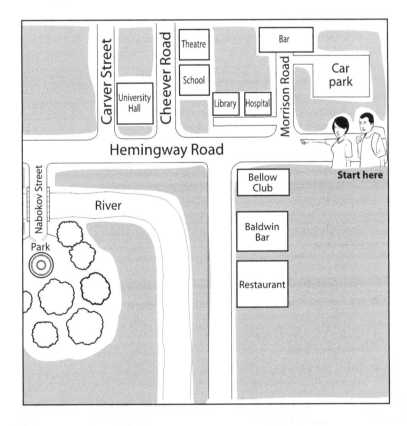

VOCABULARY
HEALTH

1 Complete the texts with the words in the box.

> running   fresh   caffeine   junk   worrying   fizzy
> vitamins   alcohol   relaxing   exercise

I have a healthy
life, I think. I buy lots
of ¹_____ fruit
and vegetables and
use these to cook
with. I don't like to
eat ²_____ food
like hamburgers or
crisps and I never drink
³_____ – not
even beer or wine.

I'm not as healthy as
I would like to be. I work in
the city and spend a lot of
time ⁴_____ about my
work. I don't eat very well
because I don't have much
time, but I make sure I get
enough ⁵_____ from
fruit and vegetables. I wish
I could spend more time
⁶_____ at home with
my family.

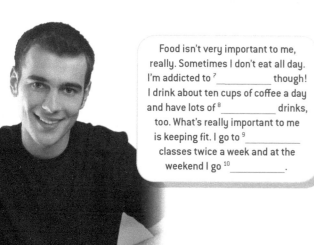

Food isn't very important to me,
really. Sometimes I don't eat all day.
I'm addicted to ⁷_____ though!
I drink about ten cups of coffee a day
and have lots of ⁸_____ drinks,
too. What's really important to me
is keeping fit. I go to ⁹_____
classes twice a week and at the
weekend I go ¹⁰_____.

GRAMMAR
PRESENT PERFECT + *FOR/SINCE*

2 Complete the conversations with the present perfect form of the verbs in brackets.

1 **A:** How long *has Carlos worked* here? (Carlos/work)
  B: About four years. He _____ here for four years. (be)

2 **A:** Did you see that comedy film last night?
  B: Yes, it was the funniest film I _____! (ever/watch)

3 **A:** Do you know where Morris _____? (go)
  B: No. I _____ him all day. (not see)

4 **A:** _____ your homework? (you/finish)
  B: No. I _____ it yet. (not start)

5 **A:** Do you know if my parcel _____? (arrive)
  B: Just a minute. I'll have a look for you.

6 **A:** _____ your watch? (you/find)
  B: Yes, it was under the sofa.

7 **A:** How long _____ Marissa? (you/know)
  B: Not very long. We _____ friends for long at all. (not be)

8 **A:** _____ my news? (you/hear)
  B: No. _____ to leave your job? (you/decide)

3 Write sentences using the prompts. Use the present perfect with *for/since*.

1 I / know / Imelda / ages
  I've known Imelda for ages.

2 he / work / for that company / six months
  _____

3 we / live / Turkey / 2013
  _____

4 I / not be / to the cinema / a long time
  _____

5 they / be here / two months now
  _____

6 I / not clean / the house / last Monday
  _____

7 she / not listen to / that music / she was a teenager
  _____

8 we / not hear / from him / he left
  _____

9 Bob / be a builder / more than forty years
  _____

10 the phone / not ring / 10 o'clock
  _____

11 I / want / to climb a mountain / I was a child
  _____

4 Underline the correct alternatives.

I = Interviewer   J = Joy

I: So, Joy, you ¹*have started/started* the Laugh to Live organisation in 2012.

J: That's right.

I: Why ²*did you start/have you started* it? What ³*did you want/have you wanted* to do?

J: I ⁴*started/have started* Laugh to Live because I ⁵*felt/have felt* I had something I wanted to share with people. In my life I ⁶*have lived/lived* and worked in four different countries, in four different continents, so ⁷*I've had/I had* a lot of experience and ⁸*I've worked/I worked* with people from all over the world.

I: And what have you learnt from these experiences?

J: I think I've learnt something very important in life. Most people just want to live a simple, happy life. But they don't know where to look for happiness. Years ago, when I ⁹*travelled/have travelled* to Africa, I ¹⁰*met/have met* poor children in the jungle who had nothing. But they had the biggest smiles ¹¹*I have ever seen/ I saw*. This taught me that happiness and laughter are inside us all. I have a few techniques which I ¹²*have used/used* to help people learn to laugh more often, especially when things are difficult in their lives. And because they now laugh more, they ¹³*have become/became* happier people.

I: Thank you, Joy. And good luck with your work.

5 **A** ▶ **6.1** Listen and tick (✓) the sentence you hear.

1 **a)** I've known her for ages.
   b) She's known it for ages.

2 **a)** They travelled a lot.
   b) They've travelled a lot.

3 **a)** He's never seen it before.
   b) He's never been here before.

4 **a)** Nothing has changed.
   b) Nothing changed.

5 **a)** I've worked in other countries.
   b) I worked in other countries.

B Listen again and repeat.

LISTENING

6 **A** ▶ **6.2** Listen to the first part of a news report and circle the correct option.

1 The reporter went to a table tennis centre for people aged _____.

   a) under fifteen   **b)** under fifty   **c)** over fifty

2 People should eat _____ portion(s) of fruit and vegetables a day.

   a) five   **b)** one   **c)** eight

3 Living a healthy life can add _____ years to your life.

   a) four   **b)** fourteen   **c)** forty

B ▶ **6.3** Listen to the whole report. Are the statements true (T) or false (F)?

1 The people at the centre play table tennis four times a week. _____

2 The first woman says playing table tennis gives her a great feeling. _____

3 Scientists studied 20,000 people for fifteen years. _____

4 They found that people who don't smoke, exercise regularly and eat lots of fruit and vegetables every day live longer. _____

5 Doctors say that only big changes to your lifestyle can help improve your health. _____

6 The second woman says she always eats five portions of fruit and vegetables a day. _____

C Read the sentences from the recording. Match the words in bold 1–5 with meanings a)–e).

1 I feel **fabulous**.

2 Scientists have now **worked out** that you can live longer if you have a healthy lifestyle.

3 They **did** some **research**.

4 People who don't smoke, who do **regular** exercise and who eat lots of fresh fruit and vegetables every day …

5 It's **part of the fun**.

a) happening once a week/once a month, etc.
b) studied something carefully to find out information
c) very good, wonderful
d) one of the things you enjoy
e) calculated

VOCABULARY
FOOD

1 Find seven types of fruit using these letters. You can use the letters more than once.

2 Complete the words in the menu and the recipe.

THE TERRACE
BISTRO MENU

CHEF'S CHOICE

Tender baby ¹ch__ck__n grilled in a ²l__m__n
and herb sauce.
Served with rice and ³br__cc__l__ .

MEAT-EATER'S DELIGHT

⁴B____fst____k marinaded in a cream
and ⁵sp__n__ch sauce.
Served with ⁶p__t__t__es.

KING'S FEAST

Roasted ⁷l__g __f l__mb with rice, ⁸c__bb__ge
and freshly steamed ⁹c____rg__tt__s.

Pasta Atlantica

- Fry 50g of ¹⁰shr__mps in a pan with a little butter.

- Add ¹¹__n____ns and ¹²g__rl__c to the pan.

- Boil 50g of ¹³m__ss__ls.

- Cook the pasta.

- Mix the pasta and seafood and put in a tray.

- Add a layer of ¹⁴ch____s__ on top and cook in the oven for twenty minutes until brown.

GRAMMAR
MAY, MIGHT, WILL

3 Circle the correct option to complete the sentences.

1 **A:** What are you doing this weekend?
   B: I'm not sure. We _____ go to the seafood restaurant.
   a) may   **b)** will   **c)** won't

2 **A:** Will that café on Wardour Street be open tomorrow?
   B: I don't know. It _____ be.
   a) will   **b)** won't   **c)** might

3 **A:** I've cooked little Johnny some vegetables for tonight's dinner.
   B: Thanks, but he _____ eat them.
   a) might   **b)** will   **c)** won't

4 **A:** Can I try your food?
   B: Be careful. It _____ be too hot for you.
   a) may   **b)** won't   **c)** may not

5 **A:** Do we need to buy any ingredients for this recipe?
   B: Maybe. We _____ have enough garlic. Can you check?
   a) won't   **b)** might not   **c)** will

6 **A:** You know Melissa's a vegetarian, don't you?
   B: OK, I _____ cook meat.
   a) won't   **b)** will   **c)** may

7 **A:** Are you going to that new bar before you leave town?
   B: I don't know. I hope so, but we _____ have time.
   a) won't   **b)** will   **c)** may not

8 **A:** What are your predictions for food in the future?
   B: The good news is I think it _____ be more healthy.
   a) won't   **b)** will   **c)** might not

4 Put the words in the correct order to make six predictions about food.

1 more / eat / know / people / what / about / will / they
   People will know more about what they eat.

2 future / we / animals / the / eat / won't / in
   _____

3 eat / food / we / more / organic / may
   _____

4 might / illegal / junk / become / food
   _____

5 fatter / people / West / will / the / get / in
   _____

6 the / left / may / there / sea / not / be / in / fish / any
   _____

READING

5 A Read the text and match pictures A–D with paragraphs 1–4.

How to eat less

*Brian Wansink of Cornell University did some **experiments** to show why we eat too much. Here are some of the results.*

1 Wansink invited a group of people to lunch. He told half of them they were eating something expensive and delicious: Royal Italian Bolognese with haricots verts. He told the other half they were eating cheap food from a can. In fact, both groups ate the same food. He secretly watched them. The ones who thought they were eating expensive food ate much more than the others.

CONCLUSION: If people think the food sounds good and is expensive, they think it tastes better.

2 Wansink did an experiment at a cinema in Chicago. He gave everyone a free bag of popcorn, but the popcorn was old and tasted bad. Most people noticed this, but they still ate almost all of it.

CONCLUSION: How much we eat depends on: where we are (in the cinema); what we are doing (**concentrating** on a film, not on food); what other people are doing (eating popcorn). These things may be more important than the taste of the food.

3 Wansink went to a sports bar and gave the customers free chicken. The waiters cleaned half the tables every few minutes and took away the chicken bones. No one cleaned the other tables. The people with clean tables ate seven pieces of chicken **on average**. The others ate five.

CONCLUSION: When we see how much we're eating, we eat less. When we can't see how much we're eating, we eat more.

4 Wansink invited people to watch a video. He gave them each a bag of sweets to eat during the film. Half the bags had sweets with seven different colours. The other bags had sweets with ten different colours. The people whose sweets had more colours ate forty-three more sweets than the others.

CONCLUSION: When there is a big **variety**, people want to try everything, so they eat more.

B Read the text again and circle the correct option.

1 Why did Wansink do the experiments?
   a) to improve the food we eat
   b) to discover why people eat more than they need
2 How did Wansink do his experiments?
   a) He asked questions about what people ate.
   b) He gave free food to people and then watched them.
3 Who ate more?
   a) the people who thought their food was expensive
   b) the people who thought their food was cheap
4 What was interesting about the popcorn experiment?
   a) The popcorn didn't taste good.
   b) The popcorn had different colours.
5 Who ate more chicken?
   a) the people with messy tables
   b) the people with clean tables
6 Who ate more sweets?
   a) the people whose sweets had seven colours
   b) the people whose sweets had ten colours

C Match the words in bold in the text with these meanings.
1 giving your attention to something   _____
2 many different types of things   _____
3 scientific tests to find information   _____
4 based on a calculation of what
   most people do

WRITING

SENTENCE STRUCTURE

6 A Join the sentences with *and, but* or *when*. Use each word twice.

1 I have always liked cooking. I cook every day.

   _____

2 I was very young. I cooked my first meal.

   _____

3 I don't eat much meat. I eat a lot of fish.

   _____

4 I was working as a chef in a horrible hotel. I decided to open my own restaurant.

   _____

5 I don't drink alcohol. I use a little wine in some of the dishes I prepare.

   _____

6 I like meeting customers at my restaurant. I ask them about the food.

   _____

B Put the words *and* and *also* in the correct place in the sentences.

1 My favourite types of food are pasta fresh fish. I like fruit.
2 Every morning I buy vegetables herbs from the market. I buy meat there.
3 I find that the food in the market is fresher better quality. It's cheaper.

VOCABULARY

ILLNESS

1 Read the clues and complete the crossword.

Across

5 It's very painful. I'm taking _____.

7 She fell down the stairs and she's _____ her leg.

9 The doctor's given me some _____ to stop the infection.

10 My arm hurts. I think I need to go to the hospital for an _____.

Down

1 We've got some _____ for your cough.

2 I don't feel well. I think I've caught a _____.

3 I'm tired. I need to get some _____.

4 He feels hot. He's got a high _____.

6 My head hurts. I've got a _____.

8 I can't speak. I've got a _____ throat.

FUNCTION

SEEING THE DOCTOR

2 Match the sentence halves.

Doctor

1 What's the	**a)** hurt?
2 How long have you	**b)** pills/antibiotics/medicine.
3 Where does it	**c)** had this problem?
4 Can I have a	**d)** worry about.
5 It's nothing to	**e)** matter?
6 I'll give you some	**f)** look?

Patient

7 I feel	**g)** about my leg.
8 It	**h)** very painful.
9 It's	**i)** sleep.
10 I'm worried	**j)** hurts when I walk.
11 I can't	**k)** sick/terrible.

3 A Some of the lines in the conversations have words missing. Write the missing word, or put a tick if the sentence is correct.

D = Doctor   P = Patient

Conversation 1

D: Good morning. How can I help? ✓

P: I'm worried my leg.

D: Your leg? What's matter with it?

P: Well, very painful. It hurts when I walk.

D: I see. How long have you the problem?

P: Since yesterday.

D: Can I a look?

P: Yes, of course.

Conversation 2

D: Hello. What's matter, Mr Smith?

P: I feel terrible.

D: All right. Where does hurt?

P: Everywhere. And I can't sleep.

D: Ah. Have you got temperature?

P: I don't know.

D: OK. Can I have look?

P: Yes, of course.

D: That's fine. It's nothing worry about.

P: But I feel terrible!

B ▶ 6.4 Listen and check.

LEARN TO

PREDICT INFORMATION

4 A Predict what the doctor says using the words in brackets.

D = Doctor   P = Patient

Conversation 1

D: Good afternoon. [1] _____ (matter)?

P: I've got a sore throat and a headache.

D: I see. [2] _____ (long)?

P: About two weeks.

D: [3] _____ (temperature)?

P: Yes. It's 38.5, so I've taken some aspirin.

D: I see. I think [4] _____ (cold). You need [5] _____ (rest) and [6] _____ (drinks).

Conversation 2

P: I think I've broken my arm.

D: Oh dear. [1] _____ (look)?

P: Yes. Here you are.

D: So, [2] _____ (where/hurt)?

P: Here, and here.

D: [3] _____ (how/do)?

P: I fell over.

D: I think you should [4] _____ (go/hospital/X-ray).

B ▶ 6.5 Listen and check.

GRAMMAR PRESENT PERFECT + EVER/NEVER OR PAST SIMPLE

1 Complete the sentences with the correct past simple or present perfect form of the verbs in brackets.

1 He ___has never travelled___ (never/travel) abroad.
2 I _____ (never/visit) Amsterdam, but I'd like to go in the future.
3 My grandparents _____ (come) to this country in 1956.
4 So far on this trip, we _____ (be) to ten countries.
5 Jane _____ (get) her exam results yesterday.
6 When you lived in Germany, _____ (you/go) to Frankfurt?
7 I hear Lindsay's girlfriend is very nice, but I _____ (not meet) her yet.
8 I _____ (not hear) you come in last night.
9 That girl started playing tennis three years ago, but she _____ (never/win) a match!
10 I know your mother likes foreign food, but _____ (she/ever/eat) snails?

GRAMMAR CAN, HAVE TO, MUST

2 Circle the correct options to complete the text.

> To enter the university library, everyone ¹_____ show a current student or staff ID. No exceptions. To borrow books, you ²_____ take the books to the front desk and show your ID. You ³_____ take out a maximum of eight books. There are some books that you ⁴_____ take out. These are marked *Reference Only*. There is a late fee of 20p per day, but you ⁵_____ renew the books online for an extra week. If you have renewed the books before the due date, you ⁶_____ pay the fee. To order books that are not in the library, you ⁷_____ fill in the form at the front desk, marked *Special Orders*. You ⁸_____ write the full title of the book, the author and the ISBN. We ⁹_____ guarantee a date for the arrival of these books. You ¹⁰_____ write in the books; anyone who is caught doing this will pay a fine.

1 a) must b) have to c) can
2 a) doesn't have to b) has to c) have to
3 a) can't b) mustn't c) can
4 a) don't have to b) can't c) have to
5 a) can b) has to c) don't have to
6 a) don't have to b) must c) can't
7 a) has to b) don't have to c) have to
8 a) can't b) must c) don't have to
9 a) doesn't have to b) can't c) has to
10 a) don't have to b) has to c) mustn't

FUNCTION GIVING ADVICE

3 Complete the conversations with words in the box.

> ~~should~~ think why suppose
> shouldn't sure should

Ella: What do you think I ¹___should___ wear to the interview? ² _____ I wear jeans?
Beth: No, you ³_____! You have to try and look smart.
Ella: I ⁴_____ so. What about this? This dress will be OK, won't it?
Beth: I'm not ⁵_____ that's a good idea. It's a bit short.
Ella: Oh yes, maybe you're right.
Beth: I ⁶_____ you should wear trousers and a jacket.
Ella: A jacket? I haven't worn a jacket since I was at school!
Beth: I've got a nice jacket. Here. ⁷_____ don't you try this on?

GRAMMAR PAST SIMPLE AND PAST CONTINUOUS

4 Underline the correct alternatives.

This story ¹*happened/was happening* while Guillermo Diaz ²*studied/was studying* English at a community college in the USA. Diaz was a very bad student who never attended classes. One evening when he ³*sat/was sitting* in a bar, he ⁴*saw/was seeing* another student, Arturo, who told him about an exam the next day. Arturo said the exam was in Room 52, but Diaz thought he said Room 62. The next day, when Diaz was doing the exam, he ⁵*realised/was realising* that he didn't know any of the answers. He tried to ask another student for the answers while the professor ⁶*didn't look/wasn't looking*, but the other student ⁷*didn't help/wasn't helping* him. The exam ⁸*had/was having* multiple-choice questions, so Diaz guessed all of the answers. A week later, while Diaz ⁹*watched/was watching* TV at home, he ¹⁰*received/was receiving* his results by post. He scored 100 percent in the exam … on American history!

GRAMMAR VERB PATTERNS

5 Each sentence has a verb missing. Complete the sentences with the infinitive or -ing form of the verbs in the box.

> ~~be~~ drive cook lose get up clean write shop

1 We expect ⅄ home by 2.30. *to be*
2 I want a great book so I can become famous!
3 I need early tomorrow, so I'm going to bed now.
4 We usually avoid at this time because of all the traffic.
5 Do you enjoy meals for large groups of people?
6 They decided the whole house after the party.
7 She loves for clothes.
8 I always seem something when I travel – usually my plane ticket!

FUNCTION ASKING FOR AND GIVING DIRECTIONS

6 Match the sentence halves.

1 The restaurant is in   a) bridge.
2 Go along   b) through the centre of town.
3 Take the   c) second right.
4 Keep going until   d) the main road.
5 You'll see the bar   e) you reach the cinema.
6 Go   f) at the corner.
7 Cross the   g) front of you.

GRAMMAR PRESENT PERFECT + FOR/SINCE

7 Cross out the incorrect alternative in each sentence.

1 They've been waiting here *since the office opened/for hours/~~since ten minutes~~*.
2 I've played the guitar *since 2012/for six years/since months*.
3 They haven't visited us *since last Christmas/for January/for several weeks*.
4 Have you known Sourav *since you were at school/for a long time/since years*?
5 I haven't eaten *for the last meal/for hours/since last night*.
6 We've lived in the USA *for a very long time/since the government changed/for now*.
7 My team hasn't won a game *for three years/since months/since they won the cup last year*.

GRAMMAR MAY, MIGHT, WILL

8 Find and correct the mistakes in the sentences.

1 I don't will go to the cinema tonight because I'm busy.
2 I may to send her an email.
3 We not might have time to go to the museum.
4 The weather report on TV said there might to be storms.
5 Joshua may not be go to the game.
6 I'm might be late to class tonight.

FUNCTION SEEING THE DOCTOR

9 A Who says phrases a)–f), the doctor (D) or the patient (P)?

a) How long have you had this problem?   _____
b) It's very painful.   _____
c) What's the problem?   _____
d) But I'm worried about missing work.   _____
e) Doctor, I feel terrible.   _____
f) Where does it hurt?   _____

B Complete the conversation with phrases a)–f) from Exercise 9A.

D = Doctor   P = Patient

D: Good morning. ¹_____
P: ²_____ I have a backache all the time and it hurts when I walk.

D: I see. ³_____
P: About two weeks.
D: Can I have a look? ⁴_____
P: Here. ⁵_____ Sometimes I can't sleep because of the pain.
D: OK, I'll give you some medicine for it. And you shouldn't do any heavy work for a few weeks.
P: ⁶_____ I'm a builder.
D: I'll write a note. OK?
P: OK. Thanks, Doctor.

C ▶ R2.1 Listen and check.

VOCABULARY REVISION

10 Write a word from Units 4–6 to match these meanings. The first letter of each word is given.

1 a_____: a school subject which involves painting and drawing
2 b_____: you look through these to see things far away
3 c_____: it's in coffee and tea and it makes you feel active
4 d_____: you make this when you decide to do something
5 e_____: a formal test
6 f_____ drink: a drink with gas
7 g_____: we play these (e.g. football, tennis)
8 h_____: students do this after school for their teacher
9 i_____ t_____: the subject of computers; what *IT* stands for
10 j_____ f_____: food that isn't healthy because it has lots of fat or sugar
11 first aid k_____: a bag of medicines, bandages, etc., to treat ill/injured people
12 l_____: books, poems, plays
13 m_____: a fast form of transport with two wheels
14 n_____: it's got empty pages and you write notes in it
15 o_____: connected to the internet
16 p_____: a small round piece of medicine that you put in your mouth and swallow
17 r_____: a sport for which you have to wear special boots with wheels
18 s_____: a large boat that carries people or things across the sea
19 t_____: an electric street train
20 u_____: special clothes that students have to wear at school
21 v_____: potatoes, carrots, onions and peas are this type of food
22 w_____: clothes that don't allow water to enter are this
23 y_____: an activity that helps relax the body and mind

CHECK

Circle the correct option to complete the sentences.

1 Everyone likes that film, but I _____ it.
a) saw   **b)** don't see   **c)** haven't seen

2 I started writing ten years ago, but I _____ anything.
a) have never published   **b)** don't publish
c) didn't publish

3 He _____ his girlfriend in 2014.
a) did meet   **b)** met   **c)** has met

4 You _____ have a passport to get into the country.
a) has to   **b)** have to   **c)** can

5 She _____ do any homework tonight so she can come with us.
a) doesn't have to   **b)** can   **c)** has to

6 You _____ see the dentist about that tooth.
a) should   **b)** try   **c)** don't

7 _____ don't you ask your friend to help you with this?
a) How   **b)** Should   **c)** Why

8 She has to _____ an appointment with a dentist.
a) start   **b)** do   **c)** make

9 He _____ too many mistakes and failed the exam.
a) made   **b)** did   **c)** wrote

10 I usually _____ new words in a dictionary.
a) study up   **b)** look up   **c)** take up

11 I _____ along the street when I met Dave.
a) walked   **b)** am walking   **c)** was walking

12 The radio was on, but nobody _____.
a) did listen   **b)** was listening   **c)** listened

13 She _____ her arm while she was skiing.
a) was broke   **b)** broke   **c)** was breaking

14 They expect _____ this game easily.
a) win   **b)** winning   **c)** to win

15 Try to avoid _____ a lot of noise because your brother is sleeping.
a) making   **b)** to make   **c)** make

16 I've decided _____ law.
a) studying   **b)** study   **c)** to study

17 Keep walking until you _____ the river.
a) at   **b)** reach   **c)** get

18 The bar is in front _____ you.
a) to   **b)** by   **c)** of

19 Did you travel _____ train?
a) on   **b)** by   **c)** the

20 You look tired – you should _____ some rest.
a) catch   **b)** make   **c)** get

21 I've known Rami _____ my first year at college.
a) since   **b)** for   **c)** because

22 She has worked with us _____ three years.
a) since   **b)** by   **c)** for

23 They haven't been here _____ 1987.
a) for   **b)** since   **c)** until

24 You _____ need a special visa, but I'm not sure.
a) will   **b)** have   **c)** might

25 In the future, cars _____ use oil because it will be too expensive.
a) will   **b)** can't   **c)** won't

26 I _____ come to the lesson because I have to work late.
a) may not   **b)** am not   **c)** will

27 You've caught a _____.
a) backache   **b)** cold   **c)** cough

28 Where does it _____?
a) sore   **b)** hurt   **c)** pain

29 I _____ yoga twice a week.
a) do   **b)** play   **c)** exercise

30 We try to _____ some exercise every day.
a) make   **b)** play   **c)** do

RESULT   /30

VOCABULARY

VERBS + PREPOSITIONS

1 Underline the correct alternatives.

1 After waiting *for/to/about* months, James decided it was the right time travel *for/to/around* the world.

2 I'm moving *to/on/in* the USA in August. At the moment I'm waiting *of/about/for* my visa.

3 I was born in Pakistan in a village with no school. I've always dreamt *in/about/for* going *to/back/from* there to open a school for the children.

4 Sal's thinking *in/to/about* doing an art course. She's looking *about/in/for* someone who can teach her how to paint.

2 Match the sentence halves.

1 When are you going	a) to Berlin because they want to be near his family.
2 I'm looking	b) for me here – I'll only be a few minutes.
3 She's travelling	c) back home? Have you booked your ticket yet?
4 He's OK. He's waiting	d) about it for a while and tell me later?
5 They moved	e) for my bag. Have you seen it anywhere?
6 Please wait	f) around America at the moment on a bus.
7 Do you want to think	g) for a friend.

GRAMMAR

USED TO

3 Complete the sentences with the correct form of *used to* and the verbs in the box.

not visit	not like	spend	not come
stay	run	study	read	be

1 We *didn't use to visit* our cousins very often when we were young.

2 I _____ a lot of books as a child, but now I only read the newspapers.

3 _____ (you) French at school?

4 There _____ a cinema in the town centre, but it's closed now.

5 _____ (you) a lot of time with your grandparents?

6 We _____ in a small hotel by the sea every summer.

7 My father was always very fit. He _____ eight kilometres every morning.

8 He _____ her because he thought she was rude. Now he's fallen madly in love!

9 Tourists _____ here very often, but now the place is very popular.

4 Read the text and look at the pictures. Then write sentences with *used to/didn't use to* using the prompts.

Ten years ago

James Turnbull and Harry Potts left their office jobs in London to move to Tobago and open a bar on the beach. Now, ten years later, they own two hotels, a restaurant and a nightclub. When James told his colleagues at work about his plans, they thought he was crazy. So when the pair opened their first bar, they called it The Crazy Bar. It's been a great success.

Now

1 James and Harry / work / London
James and Harry used to work in London.

2 they / dream / a life on the beach
_____

3 they / sit in traffic / on the way to the office
_____

4 Harry / wear / a suit to work
_____

5 James / not spend / his time / sitting on the beach
_____

6 they / not eat / tropical fruit for breakfast
_____

7 they / not wear / shorts and a T-shirt to work
_____

8 they / not go / surfing at the end of the day
_____

9 James' colleagues / think / he was crazy
_____

5 A ▶ 7.1 Listen and complete the sentences.
1 She _____ very shy.
2 I _____ a car.
3 My granddad _____ me sweets.
4 I never _____ at school.
5 They _____ in America.
6 Did you _____ to the cinema?

B ▶ 7.2 Listen and repeat. Focus on the pronunciation of *used to* and *didn't use to*.

READING

6 Read the article and match photos A–F with paragraphs 1–6.

 A
 B
 C
 D
 E
 F

BEFORE THEY WERE FAMOUS ...

1 Did you know that Brad Pitt once delivered fridges and George Clooney was a shoe salesman? If you find you are not doing very well and dream about being famous, don't give up. Some of the most famous celebrities started their working lives in some very simple jobs.

2 When Madonna first arrived in New York, looking for fame and fortune, she only had thirty-five dollars in her pocket. She took a job working at Dinky Donuts in Times Square, but later lost her job for squirting jam at one of the customers.

3 Bryan Cranston, star of TV drama Breaking Bad, worked on his grandparents' chicken farm while he was studying Political Science at university. He originally wanted to work as a police officer before he discovered he had a talent for acting.

4 Before being an actor, Johnny Depp used to sell pens. He used to telephone people to sell them pens with their names printed on them. But he didn't enjoy the job, so sometimes he tried using different voices on the telephone to make the job more interesting.

5 As a teenager, Rachel McAdams worked at a fast food restaurant during her summer holidays – for three years! It sounds like she wasn't a great employee, either, as she spent a lot of time washing her hands! 'I was not a great employee,' Rachel says. 'I broke the orange juice machine one day.'

6 Before Kanye West became famous, he worked as a sales assistant at GAP clothes shop. He raps about it in the song Spaceship from his first album, The College Dropout: Let's go back, back to the Gap!

7 Read the article again. Are the sentences true (T) or false (F)?
1 Madonna left her job at Dinky Donuts because she wanted to be famous.
2 Bryan Cranston was a police officer for many years.
3 Johnny Depp worked in sales.
4 He thought the job was boring.
5 Rachel McAdams was very good at her job at the fast food restaurant.
6 Kanye West used to sing his songs in a clothes shop.

WRITING
PARAGRAPHS

8 Read the text and number the sentences in each paragraph in the correct order.
1 introduces the main idea
2 supports the idea
3 finishes or concludes the paragraph

REACH FOR THE SKY!

___2___ Or do you dream about living the life you really want to live? The good news is that it's always possible to make changes that will improve your life.

___3___ Here are some tips.

___1___ Do you wake up in the morning excited about what the day will bring?

Set new goals

_____ What exactly do you want to change in your life?

_____ Writing down your goals is the first step towards achieving them.

_____ Decide on some new goals to help you achieve this change and write them down.

Do something different

_____ Try not doing something for a while – like not watching television for one week.

_____ This will give you time to try doing something different.

_____ Do you spend a lot of your time doing the same things every day?

Think about now

_____ If you try to focus on the present, things will seem easier.

_____ And don't worry about things which haven't happened yet.

_____ Don't spend too much time thinking about the past and worrying about decisions you have already made.

VOCABULARY

COLLOCATIONS

1 Complete the words in the news headlines.

1
KENYAN SCIENTIST
FINDS A WAY TO
C _U_ _R_ _E_ CANCER

2
FILM DIRECTOR MAKES
D_____Y ABOUT
AMAZON TRIBES

3
'HOUSE ON FIRE HERO'
S_____ THREE LIVES

4
EXCLUSIVE! FILM STAR TELLS ALL:
'HOW I B_____ FAMOUS IN
HOLLYWOOD'

5
SHOCK AS TOP LONDON LAWYER IS
A_____D FOR MURDER

6
PRINCE DECIDES TO S_____D
SIX MONTHS ABROAD

7
A HUNDRED-YEAR-OLD ACTOR PLAYS
HIS FINAL R____E IN FILM

2 Cross out the incorrect alternative in each sentence.

1 The doctor cured *the illness/medicine/Mrs Jones*.
2 This is one way to become *film/famous/successful*.
3 The killer spent *twenty years in prison/time abroad/many people*.
4 She plays *a role/a theatre/an important part in the film*.
5 In the book, Mr Travis saves *his son's life/some money/a long way*.
6 I really wanted to make a *play/film/documentary*.
7 Ms Maxwell has been arrested for *murder/thief/ a crime*.

GRAMMAR

PURPOSE, CAUSE AND RESULT

3 Find and correct the mistakes in eight of the sentences.

1 I worked hard for to pass my exams.
2 She was angry because we didn't do our homework.
3 I play a lot of sport because want to stay fit.
4 He drove for six hours to meeting you.
5 The bus was late, so that we walked.
6 I spent time abroad because of I like travelling.
7 I'm going to the restaurant for meet my friends.
8 He wanted to become a film star so he went to Hollywood.
9 I went to the shop for buying the book.
10 I live miles from my office, but so I get a train to work.

4 Complete the texts with *to*, *so* or *because*.

1 John Klimt changed his name eight times _____ he wanted to have the names of his great-grandparents. He wanted to include the women too, _____ for a short time he was called Sara, Katrina, Jessica and Margit!

2 In 2005, a town called Clark, in Texas, changed its name to Dish. Why? _____ in 2005, DISH TV network offered ten years of free satellite and digital TV to everyone if the town changed its name. _____ the town's residents agreed to do it!

3 In 2006, Australian singer Rebecca Swift changed her hair colour every day for 365 days. Why? _____ be different. She is a fan of Madonna, who changes her image all the time, _____ Rebecca copied her.

4 Epi Taione, a Tongan rugby player, changed his name to Paddy Power during the 2007 Rugby World Cup. Paddy Power is a company which gave money to the Tongan team, _____ Taione changed his name _____ say thank you!

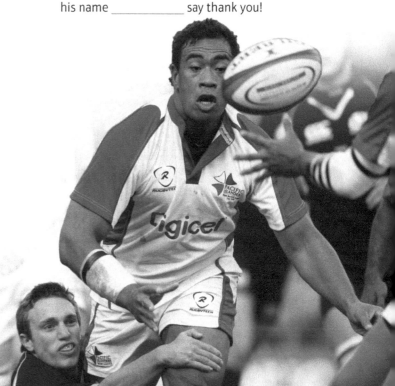

LISTENING

5 A ▶ 7.3 Listen to a radio programme and circle the correct options.

1 The programme is about people who change their _____ .
   a) job   b) nationality   c) name
2 People have _____ for changing.
   a) many reasons   b) three reasons   c) one main reason
3 Susan explains that Muhammad Ali's _____ .
   a) real name was Cassius Clay   b) first religion was Christian   c) name is Arabic
4 The programme mentions several famous _____ .
   a) sportspeople   b) writers   c) singers
5 Many people change their names when they move to a new country, especially in _____ .
   a) Europe   b) the USA and England   c) films
6 The programme mentions Angelina Jolie's _____ .
   a) childhood   b) father   c) children

Muhammad Ali

Angelina Jolie

George Michael

B Listen again and complete the notes.

- When a woman gets [1]_____ , she might want to go back to her original name.

- Cassius Clay became Muhammad Ali because he changed his [2]_____ .

- The name Freddie Mercury is probably easier to [3]_____ than Farookh Balsara.

- Another reason people want to change their name is to identify with a new [4]_____ .

- Angelina Jolie's father is an [5]_____ .

- Oprah Winfrey is called Oprah because there was a [6]_____ on her birth certificate.

C Read audio script 7.3 on page 80 and find words that match these meanings.
1 ends a marriage   _____
2 a sportsperson who fights in matches   _____
3 the person who sings the most in a band   _____
4 people who go to live in a different country   _____
5 feel that you understand or have a connection with someone or something   _____
6 stopped using   _____
7 a document that shows when and where you were born   _____

D Complete the sentences with the words in the box.

| got divorced   give an example   real name |
| lead singer   identify with   birth certificate |

1 To get a passport, you need to show your _____ .
2 I've lived in ten countries, but I don't really _____ any of them.
3 That's a good point. Can you _____ ?
4 Actor Michael Caine's _____ is Maurice Micklewhite.
5 They got married, but four years later they _____ .
6 Bono is the _____ of the band U2.

VOCABULARY
FACILITIES

1 Read the clues and complete the crossword.

Across

6 Let's meet for a coffee in the _____.

8 Professor Morris is giving a presentation in the _____ theatre at 2p.m.

9 I'm going to the _____ to borrow a book.

10 I want to buy a dictionary. I think there's a _____ over there.

Down

1 Do you know where the _____ _____ is? I need to make a photocopy of this form.

2 I need to register for my course. Is this the _____ _____?

3 I'll take you to the _____ _____. They can tell you about your accommodation.

4 When you go into the building, ask for Mr Kubovsky at the _____ _____.

5 Is there a _____ _____ near here? I need to buy a notebook.

7 Our lesson is in a different _____ today.

FUNCTION
FINDING OUT INFORMATION

2 The underlined words are in the wrong place in the conversations. Write them in the correct place.

Conversation 1
Excuse   tell

A: ¹Thank me, can you ²library me where the library is?

B: The ³reception?

A: Yes, that's right.

B: It's next to the main ⁴excuse.

A: ⁵kind you.

B: I can take you there if you like.

A: That's very ⁶tell.

Conversation 2

A: Do you ⁷opens if the cafeteria is open?

B: ⁸Thank?

A: Is the ⁹know open now?

B: Yes. I think it ¹⁰cafeteria at 8.30a.m.

A: ¹¹Sorry you.

Conversation 3

A: Excuse me. Could you ¹²classroom me?

B: Yes.

A: Can you ¹³help me where my classroom is?

B: Have you got your registration form?

A: ¹⁴tell?

B: Your registration form. ¹⁵Thank I have your registration form?

A: Yes, ¹⁶Sorry it is.

B: Your ¹⁷Can is room 401. It's over there, near the bookshop.

A: ¹⁸here you.

LEARN TO
CHECK AND CONFIRM INFORMATION

3 A Complete the responses using the clues in brackets.

1 A: It's next to the bookshop.
   B: *The bookshop*? The one near the cafeteria? (repeat key word/phrase)
   A: That's right.

2 A: You can't bring your bag into the library.
   B: So, do I have to _____ here? (rephrase)
   A: That's right.

3 A: The exam starts at 9 o'clock.
   B: Did _____? (ask a checking question)
   A: That's right.

4 A: I need to buy a notebook.
   B: _____? There's a stationery shop over there. (repeat key word/phrase)
   A: Thank you.

5 A: Can you tell me where the study centre is?
   B: It's on the left as you go out of the building.
   A: _____? (ask for repetition)
   B: It's on the left as you go out of the building.
   A: Thank you.

6 A: Where can I find Professor Adams?
   B: He's in the lecture theatre.
   A: Did _____? (ask a checking question)
   B: Yes, he's giving a presentation.

B ▶ 7.4 Listen and check.

VOCABULARY

MONEY

1 Put the letters in brackets in the correct order to complete the sentences.

1 I'm going to pay by _credit card_ (rdtcie radc).
2 I decided to pay by _____ (hasc).
3 Can you _____ (eldn) me some money?
4 Who's going to pay the _____ (libl) for this meal?
5 I usually _____ (woorbr) books from the library.
6 In my country the _____ (tosen) are green or brown and have pictures of our presidents.
7 I want a drink. Do you have any _____ (iosnc) for this machine?
8 Do you usually _____ (itp) taxi drivers in your country?
9 Lawyers _____ (rane) a lot of money.
10 She decided to _____ (nvites) her money in a small printing business.
11 How much is this painting _____ (tohrw)?
12 They bought a boat and went out to sea to _____ (thun) for _____ (searute).

2 Circle the correct options to complete the article.

MONEY TAKERS – BIG FAILURES

Steven Panjani was robbing a bank, but he needed a bag for the money. He emptied his sports bag and put the money in it. Unfortunately, he left several things in the bank, including his wallet, a bank [1] _____, a [2] _____ from the same bank, an electricity [3] _____ and his house keys. He left these on the floor of the bank and was arrested twenty minutes later.

A woman in Sri Lanka went to a company and said she wanted to [4] _____ some money in it. Then she gave them a fake $1 million [5] _____. These don't exist! The manager called the police.

A child robbed a sweet shop. He got a bag full of [6] _____, but he dropped them. He spent five minutes trying to pick them up and finished at the same time as the police arrived.

A customer at a restaurant gave the waiter his coat, but left his wallet in it. Later the waiter, Emilio Delgado, was found with $400 in [7] _____ from the wallet. When arrested, Delgado said, 'It's a [8] _____ from a customer! I [9] _____ it this afternoon!'

Willy Finn booked into a US hotel and paid by [10] _____. That night he robbed the reception. The police looked at his registration, saw his name and address, went to his house and arrested him.

1 a) cash	b) statement	c) coin
2 a) tip	b) cash	c) credit card
3 a) bill	b) cheque	c) tip
4 a) earn	b) lend	c) invest
5 a) note	b) credit card	c) ATM
6 a) receipt	b) ATMs	c) coins
7 a) cash	b) statement	c) bill
8 a) cheque	b) tip	c) coin
9 a) lent	b) earnt	c) invested in
10 a) tip	b) receipt	c) cheque

GRAMMAR

RELATIVE CLAUSES

3 Underline the correct alternatives.

1 That's the woman *who/where* works in the supermarket.
2 Hamburg is the city *who/where* Lidia went to university.
3 Is that the cake *that/who* you made for Claire's birthday?
4 Did you take the money *where/that* was on the table?
5 The hotel *where/which* we stayed on holiday was terrible.
6 Have you seen that video of the man *which/who* can eat metal?
7 Did you get the message *who/which* I sent you last night?
8 Helen is the only person I know *where/that* hates pizza.
9 That's the bar *which/where* Tina met Dan.
10 I don't like films *which/who* make me cry.

4 Join the sentences using relative clauses.

1 Callin is a private university. I studied physics there.
Callin is the private university *where I studied physics.*

2 Renata Samuels is a dentist. She fixed my teeth.
Renata Samuels is the dentist _____.

3 La Cosecha is a bar. You get free food there.
La Cosecha is a bar _____.

4 Did you get my note? I left it on your table.
Did you get the note _____?

5 Mannix Music is a shop. It sells old CDs.
Mannix Music is the shop _____.

6 Did you find the keys? I gave them to your girlfriend.
Did you find the keys _____?

7 David Bynes is a personal trainer. He helped me get fit.
David Bynes is the personal trainer _____.

8 Konstanz is a town. I was born there.
Konstanz is the town _____.

5 Find and correct the mistakes in seven of the sentences.

1 Are these the photos ⱡ *that* ~~who~~ you were looking for?
2 It's a place which you can really relax.
3 Do you still see your friend who she became a motorcycle courier?
4 Clarissa started a company that it sells organic food.
5 The book is about a girl who finds a magic forest.
6 That's the house that I was born.
7 I don't like people which talk all the time.
8 What's the name of the cake that we ate yesterday?
9 Is this the iPod that you want it?

READING

6 A Read the text. Which of these industries is *not* mentioned?

1 sports
2 music
3 food
4 films

B Read the text again and answer the questions. Who:

1 helped a football club to sell T-shirts?

_____

2 made over a million dollars for every five minutes of a film?

_____

3 made an advertisement for perfume?

_____

4 sold a business?

_____

C Find words in the text that match these meanings.

1 people who like a team and want them to win (paragraph 1) _____
2 a short or friendly name that is used by friends or family (paragraph 1)
3 boxing matches (paragraph 2) _____
4 the words an actor learns for a play or film (paragraph 3) _____
5 someone who has more than one billion dollars, pounds, euros, etc. (paragraph 4) _____

THE REAL MONEY MAKERS

Junichi Inamoto

Dr Dre

Nicole Kidman

1 When English football team Arsenal bought a Japanese player called Junichi Inamoto, the team's fans gave him a nickname: 'T-shirt'. Why? Because they thought the club bought him so that they could sell more Arsenal T-shirts in Japan. Inamoto was a very good player, but he played only five games in a year at Arsenal, none of them important. His name and face did, however, sell a lot of T-shirts.

2 These days sportspeople around the world can make lots of money without even playing. Cristiano Ronaldo, the world's highest-paid footballer in 2014, earned $80 million that year, and $28 million dollars of this was just for advertising. His weekly salary at Real Madrid was €398,000. If he played in two games a week, that was €132,666 per hour of playing! Boxer Floyd Mayweather, one of the world's highest-paid athletes, earned $105 million from just two fights.

3 Of course, it's not only football players and boxers who can make big money by the minute. Back in 1978, actor Marlon Brando played the role of Superman's father in the film Superman. He appeared for less than fifteen minutes in the film and didn't learn his lines. These had to be written on various pieces of paper around the film set! For this he earned $3.7 million. In 2004, Nicole Kidman made $2 million for a three-minute advertisement for the perfume Chanel No. 5. The company said it was a short film – a piece of art, not just an advertisement.

4 So who else has made a lot of money in a short time? Of course, there is Bill Gates and the usual businesspeople: the Walton family, who own Wal-Mart; Mexican telephone billionaire Carlos Slim Helu and Howard Stern, a US radio DJ who made about £311 a minute in 2015. And what about the music business? Perhaps surprisingly, Dr Dre has made huge sums of money, earning $620 million in 2014 after selling his headphone business for $3 billion.

VOCABULARY
MULTI-WORD VERBS

1 Read the blog entries and underline the correct alternatives.

Blame someone else!

My wife offered to look after our neighbour's dog when they went on holiday. It's a huge dog which took ¹*over / up / in* too much space in our small flat. One day we went out to the shops and left him in the flat. When we came back, he had turned the living room ²*down / up / into* a war zone! When my neighbour returned, we couldn't wait to give him ³*back / to / out*.

Rick

We started a club for people who wanted to give ⁴*in / round / up* smoking. We spent our time watching films (no smoking allowed), but after a few weeks, he took ⁵*up / back / over* the club. He loves watching films. Now we watch films seven days a week — we hardly speak to each other! We're all addicted.

Lena

2 Complete the sentences with prepositions.

1 I played squash for twenty years until I gave it _____ last year.
2 The boss offered Julia a promotion, but she turned it _____ because she wanted to spend more time with her family.
3 When are you going to give _____ that book you borrowed?
4 This desk takes _____ too much space.
5 We expected things to change after we took _____ the company.

WRITING
ADDING EMPHASIS

3 A Read the product description and put the words in brackets in the correct places.

Hanser Lightman six-string acoustic guitar: €45

• The guitar is in good condition. (very)
• It sounds good. (really)
• The guitar is easy to play. (fairly)
• It will be difficult to find a better offer than this! (extremely)

B Write a product description of one of these products in 50–100 words.

GRAMMAR
TOO MUCH/MANY, ENOUGH, VERY

4 Look at the pictures and the table. Complete the sentences with *too, much, many, enough* or *very*, and the correct names.

MELANIE

SANDRA

DORIS

	food/drink	exercise	work	TV	sleep
Melanie	spends €150 a week	30 minutes a week	44 hours a week	40 hours a week	12 hours a night
Sandra	spends €80 a week	38 hours a week	40 hours a week	no TV	8 hours a night
Doris	spends €430 a week	5 hours a week	65 hours a week	7 hours a week	4 hours a night

1 *Melanie* eats too ____*much*____ junk food.
2 _____ doesn't do _____ exercise.
3 _____ does too _____ exercise.
4 _____ doesn't sleep _____.
5 _____ sleeps _____ much.
6 _____ is _____ unhealthy.
7 _____ works too _____ hours a week.
8 _____ watches too _____ TV.
9 _____ eats _____ different types of vegetable.
10 _____ spends _____ much money on food.

5 Match the sentence halves.

1 a) There isn't enough food here; _____
  b) There's too much food here; _____
  i) we won't need all of it.
  ii) we need to buy some more.

2 a) He's too good at tennis _____
  b) He's very good at tennis _____
  i) and I love watching him play.
  ii) for us – the game will be boring if he plays.

3 a) There are too many _____
  b) There's too much _____
  i) traffic on the roads.
  ii) cars on the roads.

4 a) This film is too _____
  b) In this film there is too _____
  i) long.
  ii) much violence.

5 a) We don't have much time to catch the bus, _____
  b) We don't have enough time to catch the bus, _____
  i) so we have to be quick.
  ii) so we'll take a taxi.

6 a) The homework was very difficult, _____
  b) The homework was too difficult, _____
  i) so I didn't finish it.
  ii) but I finished it.

7 a) Oh no! I've been out in the sun too long _____
  b) I've had enough sun, _____
  i) and I'm burnt now.
  ii) so I'm going inside.

8 a) I spent too much _____
  b) I spent too many _____
  i) time relaxing, so I failed my course.
  ii) days away from my work, so I lost my job.

LISTENING

6 A ▶ **8.1 Look at the pictures, which show a true story. What do you think happened? Listen and check.**

B Listen again. Find and correct five mistakes in the summary of the story.

                                  fifty
Maggie and Joe Smith lived in the same house for ∧ ~~fifteen~~ years. When Joe died, Maggie sold the house to David Jones. A few years later, Maggie heard someone say that Jones had found some money in her old house. Jones told her there was $10,000 in the wall. He offered her $5,000. She agreed. A few days later, Jones asked Maggie to sign a contract that said she should accept $5,000 for any money found in the garden. She didn't sign it. Instead, she took Jones to court. In court, he told the truth: there wasn't $10,000. There was $15,000. Joe Smith, Maggie's husband, was putting money in the wall for fifty years and he never told his wife. In the end, the judge decided that Mr Jones should get all of the money.

VOCABULARY

SHOPPING

1 Read the clues and complete the puzzle. What's the mystery word?

```
      1 □ □ ▨ □ □
  2 □ □ □ ▨ □
      3 □ □ ▨ □
    4 □ □ □ ▨ □ □
5 □ □ □ □ ▨ □ □ □
6 □ □ □ ▨ □ □
```

1 a big shop where you can buy lots of different things: a department …

2 the particular type/name of a product (sometimes famous, e.g. Levi Jeans, Ferrari cars)

3 a period of time when shops sell their products more cheaply than usual

4 how much you pay for something

5 the opposite of *cheap*

6 a place where people buy and sell things, usually outside

Mystery word: _____

FUNCTION

BUYING THINGS

2 Put the words in the correct order to make conversations.

1 A: I / you / help / can?

_____

B: looking, / just / I'm / thanks

_____

2 A: particular / looking / you / anything / in / are / for?

_____

B: hats / you / do / sell ?

_____

3 A: these / you / larger / one / size / in / do / a / have / of?

_____

B: just / look / I'll / have / a

_____

4 A: I / on / these / try / can?

_____

B: here / yes, / the / is / room / fitting

_____

5 A: card / you / cash / are / by / credit / or / paying?

_____

B: card / credit / by

_____

6 A: you / PIN / your / enter / can?

_____

B: of / yes, / course

_____

3 Complete the text with one word in each gap.

" When I started in 1968, everything was different. Most people paid by [1]_____ because credit cards weren't very common. Now you have to ask them to enter their [2]_____ or [3]_____ their name. Shops were much smaller in those days, too. If a customer was looking for something in [4]_____, like a dress in a special colour, or if the shoes didn't [5]_____ and they needed a smaller [6]_____, we found it for them. And you knew most of your customers. These days the first thing you say is, '[7]_____ I help you?' In those days it was, 'Hello, John. How are you?' "

LEARN TO

DESCRIBE THINGS

4 Underline the correct alternatives.

1 A: Excuse me. I'm looking for one of those *stuff/things* you use to open cans.

B: You mean a can opener? They're just over there.

2 A: Excuse me. Do you have any of that *stuff/things* for taking paint off walls?

B: You mean paint stripper? We have some just here.

3 A: I'm looking for some fusilli. It's *type/a type* of pasta.

B: Oh, I'm afraid we're out of stock.

4 A: Do you have any books by Malcolm Gladwell? He's *kind a/a kind of* journalist.

B: Oh yes. They're in the *Popular Psychology* section.

LISTENING

5 A ▶ 8.2 Listen and match A–D with conversations 1–4.

B Listen again and answer the questions.

1 In conversation 1, what does the customer want?

_____

2 In conversation 2, what two things does the shop assistant show the customer? _____ ,

_____

3 In conversation 3, does the shop assistant find what he's looking for? _____

4 In conversation 4, how does the customer pay?

_____

VOCABULARY

NATURE

1 Complete the nature words in the quiz. Then do the quiz and check your answers at the bottom.

---

1 The world's largest __c__ __n is
   a) the Pacific.   **b)** the Atlantic.

2 The Gobi D__s__rt is in
   a) Australia.   **b)** Asia.

3 The m__ __nt__ __n r__ng__ where you can find Mount Everest is called
   a) the Andes.   **b)** the Himalayas.

4 The second longest r__v__r in the world is
   a) the Amazon.   **b)** the Nile.

5 At over 1,700 m deep, the deepest l__k__ in the world is
   a) Baikal.   **b)** Victoria.

6 The highest w__t__rf__ll in the world is
   a) Niagara Falls.   **b)** Angel Falls.

Answers: 1 a, 2 b, 3 b, 4 b, 5 a, 6 b

GRAMMAR

COMPARATIVES/SUPERLATIVES

2 Look at the table and complete the sentences comparing France and Poland. Use the words in brackets.

	France	Poland
Population	64 million people	38 million people
Size	548,000 square km	313,000 square km
Highest mountain	4,810 m (Mont Blanc)	2,499 m (Rysy)
Average temperature (January)	3°C	-3°C
Average temperature (July)	23°C	19°C

1 The population in France is ___bigger than___ the population in Poland. (big)

2 Poland is _____ France. (small)

3 Mont Blanc in France is _____ Rysy in Poland. (high)

4 In January it is _____ than in France. (cold)

5 In July it is _____ than in Poland. (hot)

3 A ▶ **9.1** Listen and circle the correct stress pattern.
   a) oOo   **b)** Ooo   **c)** ooO

B Listen again and repeat.

C ▶ **9.2** Listen and check your answers to Exercise 2. Then listen again and repeat.

4 Complete the sentences with the comparative or superlative form of the adjectives in brackets.

1 It's been _____ (cold) winter in thirty years.

2 The weather is getting _____ (bad).

3 It's _____ (popular) tourist destination in the country.

4 It's _____ (cheap) to stay in a bed and breakfast than to stay in a hotel.

5 People are working _____ (long) hours than before.

6 The summers are much _____ (hot) than they were.

7 In the winter, the days are _____ (short).

8 This sauce tastes _____ (good) than the other one you made.

9 We've been on _____ (long) journey of our lives.

10 This is _____ (happy) day of my life!

11 It's _____ (funny) programme I've ever watched.

12 The exam was _____ (difficult) than I expected.

READING

5 Look at the reasons for growing your own vegetables. Then read the text. Which reasons are mentioned?

1 It's a good way to relax.
2 The food tastes better when you grow it yourself.
3 It's cheaper than buying food in the supermarket.
4 It's a good way to earn some extra money.

MAKING THE WORLD A GREENER PLACE: GROW YOUR OWN VEGETABLES!

We meet people from around the world who enjoy growing their own food.

UNITED STATES

When you think of Washington, you might not think of vegetable patches, but there are lots of them. 'Community plots' where people can grow their own food are getting more popular. Brian Wallis, who works in banking, likes gardening in his free time. And he's not alone. 'When you work in the city, gardening is a great way to relax,' he says.

AUSTRALIA

Outside Sydney there are more than fifty community gardens. In the garden at the Addison Road Centre people grow all kinds of things, from bananas to coffee, herbs, beans and vegetables. They also have lemon, peach and cherry trees. People come here to learn new skills related to organic gardening and recycling.

KENYA

In Kenya having a piece of land to grow food on is not just a good way to relax, it's a way to earn some extra money. Maxwell shares the land his father gave him with his six brothers. They grow bananas, coffee and sugar on the land, as well as vegetables to eat at home. 'Some of the food we eat ourselves,' he says, 'and some we sell at the market.'

RUSSIA

Every weekend in the summer, the roads of Russia's big cities are full of traffic, with families escaping to their 'dacha'. A 'dacha' can be anything from an old shed in a field to a huge house in the countryside, but the reason they go is the same. People from the city can enjoy the fresh air and grow some vegetables. Tatiana, who has a plot near the Black Sea, grows tomatoes and cucumber in the summer and cabbage in the winter. 'It always tastes much better when you grow it yourself,' she says.

6 Read the text again and answer the questions.

1 Why does Brian Wallis think people enjoy gardening?

_____
_____
_____

2 What can people learn at the Addison Road Centre, outside Sydney?

_____
_____
_____

3 How did Maxwell get his land?

_____
_____
_____

4 What do Maxwell and his brothers do with the food they grow?

_____
_____
_____

5 What is a 'dacha' in Russia?

_____
_____
_____

6 What can people who live in Russian cities enjoy at their 'dacha'?

_____
_____
_____

WRITING
SIMILAR SOUNDING WORDS

7 Find and correct the spelling mistakes in the sentences.

1 Is this you're coat?
2 They gave us there car for the weekend.
3 Have you got an extra ticket? I'd like to come to.
4 We spent the weekend by the see.
5 Do you know wear the office is?
6 Are you sure this is the write way?

8 Underline the correct alternatives.

How often do you use [1]*you're/your* car? I try to use mine as little as possible. I walk or use my bike to get around. I live in a small city though, so [2]*it's/its* quite easy. And it keeps me fit [3]*two/too*. If I want to go to the [4]*see/sea* for the weekend, or something like that, then I usually get the bus or the train. I don't think people should spend so much time in [5]*there/their* cars. It's not [6]*write/right*.

VOCABULARY
THE OUTDOORS

1 A Find eight words connected with the outdoors in the puzzle.

F	E	A	T	U	R	E	S	C
N	D	E	R	F	S	G	C	O
A	I	R	O	Y	Z	A	E	R
T	S	T	P	A	R	K	N	U
U	D	E	I	F	C	X	E	R
R	S	F	C	O	P	L	R	A
A	D	N	A	M	E	W	Y	L
L	W	I	L	D	L	I	F	E

B Complete the phrases with words from Exercise 1A.

1 geographical _____
2 fresh _____
3 national _____
4 beautiful _____
5 _____ centre
6 _____ rainforest
7 _____ area
8 _____ beauty

C Complete the sentences with phrases from Exercise 1B.

1 We live in a polluted city, but in the countryside near us you can breathe _____.
2 I hate cities. I prefer living in a _____ because I grew up on a farm.
3 Unfortunately, the _____ was closed, so we didn't see the rare birds.
4 Mountains, waterfalls and volcanoes are examples of _____ you can find on this continent.
5 The Amazon is the world's biggest _____; it has incredible plant life because of all the rain.
6 Our biggest _____ is Etosha. You can drive around it and see wild animals.
7 We went for a walk in the hills. Then we stopped to take photos of the _____.
8 The Cotswolds is an area of _____. It's very green.

GRAMMAR
ARTICLES

2 Complete the sentences with the words in the box and add *a*, *an*, *the* or – (no article).

January	doctor	weather	Europe	architect
camera	~~right~~	elephants	noise	Thursday	sun

1 My house is on ___the right___.
2 It's so cold in Iceland! I really hate _____.
3 During our safari in Namibia we saw lots of _____.
4 He loved buildings and wanted to be _____.
5 I bought a camera and a bag. Then we went travelling and I dropped and broke _____.
6 When I was twenty, I travelled around _____.
7 I'm working in December, but I'll be on holiday in _____.
8 Let me see him! I can help. I'm _____.
9 We didn't have a map to guide us, so we used _____.
10 Bye! See you on _____.
11 I heard a small noise. After a while, _____ got louder.

3 Complete the book review with *a*, *an*, *the* or – (no article).

A Walk on the Wild Side
by Giuseppe de Luca

Giuseppe de Luca has been [1] ___an___ adventurer all his life. He once ran away from home in [2] _____ Sicily and survived on fish that he caught from [3] _____ river with his hands. De Luca's book explains why he can't do [4] _____ normal job. He has tried office work, building boats, driving lorries across Europe and looking for dinosaur bones in [5] _____ Kenya. He couldn't do any of these for more than [6] _____ few months. He finally finds happiness living on [7] _____ smallest beach in Papua, New Guinea. But then he has some [8] _____ problems with the local police and they send him back to Sicily. Why is his story so interesting? It's his humour and his innocence. He is shy with girls. He doesn't have [9] _____ email address and he has never touched [10] _____ mobile phone. He clearly loves living alone in [11] _____ wild and his book makes a great companion.

LISTENING

4 A ▶ 9.3 Listen and match statements a)–d) with speakers 1–4.

a) He/She has spent a lot of time in the garden. _____
b) He/She lives on a farm. _____
c) He/She lives near a beach. _____
d) He/She comes from the USA. _____

B Listen again and answer the questions. Do not use more than three words for each answer.

1 **a)** Who does the speaker go for walks with these days?

_____

  b) What did she see on the beach once?

_____

2 **a)** What did the speaker invent as a child?

_____

  b) Where does she say she 'grew up'?

_____

3 **a)** When does the speaker go hiking and camping?

_____

  b) What 'big' things does he say that Americans like?

_____

4 **a)** What animals does the speaker work with?

_____

  b) What doesn't he like about living on a farm?

_____

C Match the words and phrases in bold in 1–8 with meanings a)–h).

1 That was **fun**. _____
2 It was **enormous**. _____
3 I played in a **tree house**. _____
4 You could **be outside** all day. _____
5 I go **hiking**. _____
6 There are **all kinds of** plants and animals. _____
7 It's **completely normal** to see animals around. _____
8 I really like **feeding** the pigs. _____

a) walking in the countryside
b) very common
c) giving food to
d) enjoyable
e) many different types of
f) a small house in a tree, usually for children
g) extremely big
h) be in the open air, not in a building

D Read what Gyorgi says about his experiences in nature. Complete the text with the words and phrases in bold in Exercise 4C.

'When I was younger, I lived in a very cold part of Russia. It was
¹_____ for the temperature to be minus twenty degrees and in the winter, you might not
²_____ for many weeks. We spent a lot of time at home, playing games and singing in front of the fire. To be honest, it wasn't much
³_____ in winter, but in summer we did ⁴_____ enjoyable activities. Where I lived, there were some mountains and forests and we sometimes went ⁵_____ in the mountains with my parents. And I remember we once built a
⁶_____ in my garden. My brother loved birds and he spent hours
⁷_____ them different types of fruit and nuts while he was sitting in it. As a child, I always thought our garden was ⁸_____, but when I went back there a few years ago, I saw that it was quite small.'

VOCABULARY
ANIMALS

1 Look at the photos and complete the puzzle. What's the mystery word?

Mystery word: _____

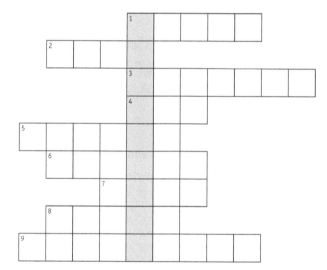

FUNCTION
MAKING GUESSES

2 Find and correct the mistakes in five of the sentences.
1. That animal might to be a chimpanzee or a monkey.
2. Maybe that's a glacier in the photo.
3. The waterfall don't can be here – it's too dry.
4. That bird can't be an eagle – it's too small.
5. Perhaps that the people scared all the animals away.
6. The mountain range in the picture could to be the Himalayas.
7. Those might be a bear's footprints on the ground.
8. That's definitely no a mosquito bite – it's too big.

3 Underline the correct alternatives.
1. The rainforest is home to thirty percent of all animal and plant life on Earth and 2.5 million types of insects. But it is disappearing because people cut down the trees for money. We don't know how fast it is disappearing, but satellite pictures show that it *might/definitely* be 15,000 km every year. Some scientists think the rainforest *could/can't* disappear completely by 2080.
2. We aren't sure exactly how many people died during the tsunami, but it was *might/perhaps* as many as 1,000. The tsunami destroyed large parts of the city and the complete reconstruction of houses and other buildings *can't/might* take ten years or more.
3. Everyone knows Venice – it *can't/might* be Italy's most famous city – but now it has a big problem: being built on water, it is now sinking into the water. The situation is very serious: *maybe/could* Venice will be completely under water in the next sixty years.
4. Because of global warming, the ice is melting in the Arctic and some scientists say there *can't/might* be no ice there by 2060. Many animals that live in the Arctic, for example polar bears and foxes, *could/perhaps* be in danger.

LEARN TO
GIVE YOURSELF TIME TO THINK

4 Put the letters in brackets in the correct order to complete the conversations.
1. **A:** Are you coming to the party tonight?
   B: _____ (lelw), I hope so. But I have a lot of homework to do.
2. **A:** How do you stop this machine?
   B: _____ (ahtt's a odgo eisunotq). Perhaps it's that button there.
3. **A:** Who do you think is going to win?
   B: _____ (ti's dhra ot yas). But Manchester United are a great team.
4. **A:** Where were you yesterday at 4.00?
   B: _____ (tel em ntkih). I was at home!
5. **A:** How old is Lina?
   B: _____ (ml' tno eurs). Maybe thirty? Or thirty-five?

GRAMMAR USED TO

1 Complete the second sentence using *used to*. Write two words in each gap. Contractions count as two words.

1 I went to the cinema every week when I was a student. Now I hardly ever go.
I used to go to the cinema a lot.

2 William paints every day. He never did this before.
William _____ use to paint every day.

3 I drank fizzy drinks all the time when I was younger. Now I never drink them.
I used _____ fizzy drinks all the time.

4 These days she reads a lot. In the past she read very little.
She didn't _____ read much.

5 I recognise that woman. Did she live near us?
Did _____ to live near us?

6 When I was young, I played the guitar, violin, drums and flute. Now I don't play anything.
I used _____ lots of musical instruments.

7 I remember your cousins. Did they visit you regularly years ago?
_____ cousins use to stay with you?

8 My father always called me 'Princess' when I was a child. Now he calls me by my real name.
My father _____ call me 'Princess' when I was little.

9 I hated classical music when I was a teenager. Now I love it.
I didn't _____ like classical music.

10 When I was younger, I was a teacher. Now I'm a tour guide.
I used _____ a teacher.

GRAMMAR PURPOSE, CAUSE AND RESULT

2 Complete the sentences with *so*, *to* or *because*.

1 Sarah was unhappy *because* I forgot her birthday.

2 I ate the bread _____ I was hungry.

3 The tickets were too expensive, _____ we didn't go to the concert.

4 Yuko was ill, _____ she didn't come to class.

5 Ben went to Liberia _____ make a documentary.

6 She was unhealthy _____ she smoked and ate fatty foods.

7 I bought a money belt _____ keep my passport and cash safe.

8 It was really hot, _____ Pilar wore her sunhat.

9 They are here _____ take an exam.

10 I went to the shops _____ buy some milk.

11 Sandra was cold and tired, _____ she went home.

12 Jacob didn't buy anything _____ he didn't have any money.

FUNCTION FINDING OUT INFORMATION

3 A Add the missing letters and write the sentences.

1 Cld u hlp me?
_____

2 Cn u tll me whr th offc is?
_____

3 Whr cn I fnd a pst offc?
_____

4 Wht tm ds th lbrry opn?
_____

5 Whn do th lssns strt?
_____

6 Is th swmmng pl opn on Sndys?
_____

7 I nd t spk t th director of studies.
_____

B ▶ R3.1 Listen and check.

VOCABULARY REVISION

4 Complete the conversations with the words in the box.

documentary	cure	about	moves	for
spent	back	travel	desk	room

1 A: I'm thinking _____ becoming a doctor.
B: So you can _____ people?

2 A: I _____ a year abroad after university. I went to Spain, Italy and Poland.
B: That sounds great! I'd love to _____ around Europe.

3 A: Oh no! I left my book in the photocopying _____.
B: You'll have to go _____ and get it.

4 A: Excuse me. Where's the registration _____?
B: I don't know. I'm also looking _____ it!

5 A: I hear that film director is making a _____.
B: Yes. It's about a British woman who _____ to the Amazon rainforest.

GRAMMAR RELATIVE CLAUSES

5 Complete the sentences with the phrases in the box. Use relative clauses.

we drove to California   my son was born
you work quietly or borrow books
builds his own hospital in India
designs computer systems for businesses

1 The programme is about a Swiss doctor *who builds his own hospital in India*.

2 That's the car _____.

3 France is the country _____.

4 I work for an IT company _____.

5 A library is a place _____.

GRAMMAR TOO MUCH/MANY, ENOUGH, VERY

6 Underline the correct alternatives.

1 **A:** Do we have enough rice?
   B: Enough? We have far too *many/much/very*!

2 **A:** Do you want some more to eat?
   B: No, thanks. I've eaten *much/many/enough*.

3 **A:** What do you think of this photographer?
   B: I think she's *much/enough/very* good.

4 **A:** Do you like your new house?
   B: Not really. It's *too/much/many* small for six people.

5 **A:** Are you enjoying life in the city?
   B: It's OK, but we don't have *much/very/many* friends.

6 **A:** Shall we study here?
   B: No. There's too *many/much/very* noise.

7 A Find and correct the mistakes in the sentences.

1 Excuse me. Do you to sell binoculars? _____
2 Do you have one these in a larger size? _____
3 Are you looking for anything in particularly? _____
4 It isn't fitting me. _____
5 Can you just to sign here, please? _____
6 Where's the fit room? _____

B Who says the sentences in Exercise 7A: the customer (C) or the sales assistant (S)?

VOCABULARY MONEY; MULTI-WORD VERBS; SHOPPING

8 Underline the correct alternatives.

1 Which means 'give money to someone for a short time': *lend* or *borrow*?
2 Which are made of paper: *notes* or *coins*?
3 Which means 'put money in a company': *invest in* or *earn*?
4 Which do you do when you buy a company: *take over* or *take back*?
5 Which means 'stop doing something': *give back* or *give up*?
6 Which can be outside on the street: *a department store* or *a market*?

GRAMMAR COMPARATIVES/SUPERLATIVES

9 Put the words in the correct order to make sentences.

1 elephants / lions / are / than / bigger
   _____

2 gold / silver / than / cheaper / is
   _____

3 this / years / is / for / weather / worst / the / many
   _____

4 Russia / world / largest / the / in / is / the / country?
   _____

5 a / than / more / Mercedes / Toyota / expensive / is / a
   _____

GRAMMAR ARTICLES

10 Complete the text with *a*, *an*, *the* or – (no article).

[1] __A__ plane carrying [2]_____ actor, [3]_____ politician, a monk and a cleaner is going to crash. There are only [4]_____ three parachutes. [5]_____ actor says, 'I entertain [6]_____ millions of people, so I should live.' He takes one of [7]_____ parachutes and jumps out of [8]_____ plane. The politician says, 'I'm [9]_____ most intelligent person in [10]_____ England, so I should live. He also takes [11]_____ parachute and jumps. The monk says, 'I'm [12]_____ old man and I have lived [13]_____ good long life. You take [14]_____ last parachute.' The cleaner says, 'Don't worry. The most intelligent man in [15]_____ country just jumped out with my [16]_____ rucksack on his back!'

FUNCTION MAKING GUESSES

11 Cross out the incorrect alternatives.

1 **A:** Is that Richard in the photo?
   B: He has the same hair colour, but I'm not sure. It *could/can't/might be* him.

2 **A:** Are you going to the meeting tomorrow?
   B: I don't really know. *Maybe/I definitely will/Perhaps*.

3 **A:** What's the answer to question 3?
   B: I don't know, but *it can't be/it's definitely not/it mightn't be* c, because Moscow is in Russia.

4 **A:** Is Paris as expensive as London?
   B: It *could/can't/might* be. When I went there a few years ago, I paid €12 for a coffee!

5 **A:** Why hasn't she moved to a place nearer work?
   B: I don't know, but *it can't be/perhaps it's/it might be* too expensive.

VOCABULARY NATURAL PLACES, THE OUTDOORS, ANIMALS

12 Write the words in the box in the correct column.

whale   monkey   fresh air   ocean   pigeon   shark
dolphin   coastline   eagle   geographical features
cheetah   wildlife centre   mosquito   lake   bear

natural places/the outdoors	land animals	animals that fly	animals that live in water

CHECK

Circle the correct option to complete the sentences.

1 I _____ to live in Valladolid in Spain.
    a) was   **b)** use   **c)** used

2 She didn't _____ to smoke.
    a) used   **b)** regularly   **c)** use

3 Who did you _____ to play with when you were a child?
    a) use   **b)** using   **c)** used

4 I studied for six years _____ become a doctor.
    a) so   **b)** to   **c)** for

5 I borrowed some money _____ I wanted to buy a car.
    a) because   **b)** for   **c)** so

6 The lecture was boring, _____ we left early.
    a) because   **b)** why   **c)** so

7 This is _____ important problem at the moment.
    a) the least   **b)** more   **c)** least

8 _____ you tell me where the housing office is?
    a) Shall   **b)** Could   **c)** Do

9 One day I'm going to travel _____ the world.
    a) everywhere   **b)** on   **c)** around

10 He wanted to _____ famous.
    a) become   **b)** make   **c)** have

11 This is the shop _____ I worked for ten years.
    a) that   **b)** what   **c)** where

12 She's the woman _____ gave me a fifty-dollar tip last week.
    a) which   **b)** who   **c)** how

13 This is the restaurant _____ serves terrible frozen food.
    a) who   **b)** what   **c)** that

14 I don't do _____ exercise.
    a) a lot   **b)** enough   **c)** too

15 There are still some trams in San Francisco, but not _____.
    a) much   **b)** very   **c)** many

16 I can't close my bag because I bought _____ many souvenirs!
    a) too   **b)** enough   **c)** very

17 Can I try _____ these jeans?
    a) on   **b)** in   **c)** up

18 This shirt doesn't _____.
    a) right   **b)** fitting   **c)** fit

19 Can you _____ me some money?
    a) do   **b)** lend   **c)** borrow

20 She gave _____ eating meat last year.
    a) up   **b)** out   **c)** back

21 That was the _____ meal I've ever eaten.
    a) good   **b)** best   **c)** better

22 Jane is _____ before.
    a) the happier   **b)** the happiest   **c)** happier than

23 Your boat is _____ beautiful than ours.
    a) the   **b)** most   **c)** more

24 At a party yesterday I met _____ who knows you.
    a) man   **b)** a man   **c)** the man

25 My dog is always barking at _____.
    a) a moon   **b)** moon   **c)** the moon

26 She's _____ best player in the team.
    a) the   **b)** a   **c)** most

27 We _____ go to Spain this summer, but we aren't sure.
    a) definitely   **b)** might   **c)** maybe

28 _____ Harry can help you with this exercise.
    a) Perhaps   **b)** He might   **c)** It's definitely

29 It's one of the biggest mountain _____ in the world.
    a) lines   **b)** places   **c)** ranges

30 I used to live in a _____ area, far from the city.
    a) rural   **b)** wildlife   **c)** park

RESULT   /30

VOCABULARY
DESCRIBING A CITY

1 Add vowels to complete the words.

1 There's a lot of tr__ff__c.
2 It's very cr__wd__d.
3 The streets are cl__ __n and s__f__.
4 I love the n__ghtl__f__.
5 There are lots of th__ngs t__ s__ __ and d__.
6 The p__bl__c tr__nsp__rt syst__m is excellent.
7 In the city centre, there's quite a lot of cr__me.
8 I usually find people are fr__ __ndly and p__l__t__.
9 There are some lovely parks and gr__ __n sp__c__s.
10 Some of the old b__ __ld__ngs are beautiful.

2 Complete some people's descriptions of their cities. Use the phrases in brackets to help you.

1 'There are lots of beautiful _____, like the museums and the cathedral.' (places like houses, with walls and a roof)
2 'The _____ _____ system is great. It's really cheap.' (buses, trams and underground)
3 'It's a problem in the morning because there's a lot of _____.' (a lot of cars)
4 'People are always very _____ and _____.' (stop to talk or help you; say things like *please* and *thank you*)
5 'The thing I like best is the parks. There are lots of _____ _____ where you can go for a walk or sit and enjoy the view.' (places with trees and plants)
6 'The problem is that there's a lot of _____.' (illegal activity)
7 'It's an industrial city, so it's very _____.' (the air and water are not clean)
8 'I don't like going into the city because it's very _____.' (too many people in a small space)
9 'It has a great _____ with lots of clubs staying open all night long.' (places to go out at night)
10 'I like it where I live. The streets are _____ and _____.' (no rubbish; crime)

GRAMMAR
USES OF *LIKE*

3 Complete the conversations using phrases with *like*.

1 **A:** Did you choose the salmon starter? What's _____?
   B: It's delicious. Try some.
2 **A:** Do _____ classical music?
   B: No, I can't stand it. I only listen to rock.
3 **A:** What _____ doing at the weekend?
   B: Nothing much. We like staying at home and relaxing!
4 **A:** What _____ your weekend _____?
   B: It was great. We went out on Saturday and had a really good time.
5 **A:** I haven't met your sister. What's _____?
   B: She's really funny. I'm sure you'll like her.
6 **A:** _____ the weather _____ at the moment?
   B: It's raining, as usual.
7 **A:** _____ living in London?
   B: I love it. There are so many things to see and do.
8 **A:** What _____ that new restaurant by the river _____?
   B: It's lovely. We ate there last week.

4 A Find and correct the mistakes in the questions. Add, cross out or change a word.

1 **A:** What's your new be teacher like?
   B: She's really good. She makes the lessons interesting.
2 **A:** What's it to like living in the country?
   B: It's a bit quiet. I think I preferred the city.
3 **A:** Does your mother staying with you?
   B: She loves it. She comes to stay once a month.
4 **A:** Are you like eating out in restaurants?
   B: I enjoy it sometimes, but I prefer to cook at home.
5 **A:** Is it much more expensive to live there now? What the prices like?
   B: It's not too bad. But it's more expensive than it was.
6 **A:** Do your brother like it in Scotland?
   B: He likes it a lot. He says it's beautiful.
7 **A:** Which's your new job like? Are you enjoying it?
   B: It's brilliant. The people I work with are really friendly.

B ▶ 10.1 Listen and check.

▶ 10.2 Listen and repeat.

Where is the city of love?

Which is the most romantic city in the world? Which is the cheapest? We've travelled around the world to find the cheapest, most romantic and safest cities. Can you find your perfect destination?

1 The world's most romantic city

Paris is the city of love. Most Europeans think Paris is the most romantic city in Europe, although Vienna, Prague and Venice are popular, too. So what's the most romantic thing you can do in Paris? Well it's not go to the top of the Eiffel Tower – that's too crowded. Buy some bread and cheese and enjoy a picnic near the river. Or spend the afternoon sitting outside a pavement café, just watching the people go by. Paris is perfect for couples.

2 The cheapest city in the world

Mumbai in India is the least expensive city in the world. Twice a year there is a list made which compares the cost of living in different cities around the world, and cities like Moscow, London and Tokyo are always at the top. However, Mumbai is at the bottom of the list, giving it the title of the cheapest city in the world to live in.

3 The safest city

Did you know that New York is now one of America's safest big cities? There is less crime now and what was once one of the most dangerous cities in the world is not any more. This is good news for the 55 million visitors who come to New York every year for the great shopping, the museums, some of the best restaurants in the world and, of course, to see the Statue of Liberty, Times Square and other famous sights.

READING

5 Try to guess the answers to the questions. Then read the text to check.

1 Which city is called the most romantic city in the world by more than fifty percent of Europeans?
2 Which is the cheapest city to live in?
3 Which statement about New York is true?
  a) It's one of the safest big cities in the USA.
  b) It's one of the most dangerous cities in the USA.

6 Read the text again and answer the questions.

1 Do people think that Vienna is a romantic city?
2 What's the problem with going to the Eiffel Tower?
3 According to the article, are Moscow, London and Tokyo expensive cities to live in?
4 Has New York always been a safe city?
5 How many people visit New York every year?
6 What are two famous sights in New York?

7 Find words in the text that match these meanings.

1 that many people like (paragraph 1)
2 a meal you eat outside, especially in the countryside (paragraph 1)
3 walk past (paragraph 1)
4 the price of things like food, bills and public transport (paragraph 2)
5 at some time in the past (paragraph 3)
6 things that tourists visit in a city (paragraph 3)

WRITING

USING FORMAL EXPRESSIONS

8 Put the words in the correct order to write an email.

1 Mr / Smith, / dear
2 ask / college / am / courses / I / at / to / about / your / writing
3 you / know / have / I / would / to / in / like / August / courses / what
4 this, / prices / addition / to / in / know / the / like / I / to / would
5 soon / to / I / from / forward / you / look / hearing
6 sincerely, / Bridges / yours / Sally

9 Write an email (80–100 words) asking for information about the accommodation in the advertisement.

Host family accommodation available for students. Please email Sam Wellings for further details.

Sam Wellings, Accommodation Officer

email: SWellings@1email1.com

VOCABULARY
CRIME AND PUNISHMENT

1 Complete the words in the sentences.
1 The p__l__ce __ff__c__r caught the th__f.
2 The j__dg__ gave her a long pr__s__n s__nt__nc__.
3 A lot of sh__pl__ft__rs st__l mobile phones.
4 The cr__m__n__l knew the v__ct__m.
5 He was given a f__n__ for wr__t__ng gr__ff__t__ on a wall.
6 C__mm__n__ty s__rv__c__ isn't a good punishment for a crime like fr__d.
7 Last year he was __rr__st__d for sh__pl__ft__ng.
8 The police are __nv__st__g__t__ng the th__ft of a famous painting.
9 In the film, he br__ks into a bank and sh__ts a guard.

GRAMMAR
PRESENT/PAST PASSIVE

2 Match the sentence halves.
1 Over 4,000 foxes are ____
2 Our academic courses are ____
3 This type of clothing is ____
4 Until recently, charity workers weren't ____
5 The buildings were ____
6 Animal fat isn't ____
7 The thief was ____
8 That window wasn't ____

a) used in our food.
b) made in our factory in Milan.
c) paid much money for their work.
d) killed every year for their fur.
e) taken to prison.
f) broken by my boys.
g) designed by French architects.
h) recognised by colleges all over the world.

3 Underline the correct alternatives.

My favourite crime programme is CSI, an American series. Usually, it has the same structure. Firstly, someone ¹*kills/is be killed/is killed* mysteriously. After this, the CSI officers ²*are called/call/are call* to solve the mystery. They collect evidence which ³*looks/is looked/is look* at very carefully in the laboratory. Then the CSI officers ⁴*are brought/have brought/bring* various people to their office and ask questions. More evidence ⁵*has discovered/discovers/is discovered* which allows the CSI officers to find the killer.

So, why do I like it? The most interesting thing is the way the evidence ⁶*is found/has found/is find*. They never ⁷*are missed/miss/are miss* anything – a hair, a contact lens, even a dead insect. I also like the characters of the CSI officers. They are not perfect people, but they ⁸*are done/do/were done* their job perfectly.

4 Complete the texts with the past simple active or passive form of the verbs in the box.

| tell choose say catch give come |
| arrest have |

A girl in North Carolina ¹_____ for theft. During her trial, she ²_____ to go home and get her favourite possession. She ³_____ back with her iPod. The judge threw it onto the floor and broke it. 'Now you know how it feels to lose your favourite possession,' he said. 'Don't do it to anybody else.'

William Brown, aged nineteen, ⁴_____ stealing a TV from a house. Brown said the TV was for his little brother, who ⁵_____ a broken leg and was bored in bed. The judge sentenced Brown to no TV-watching for a year. Amazingly, the victim of the crime ⁶_____, 'It's OK. I have two TVs. He can borrow one while his brother gets better.'

Lucas Stepanovich drove through town playing loud music with his windows down. At his trial, he ⁷_____ a choice: pay a $100 fine or listen to loud classical music for six hours. He ⁸_____ the music.

5 Complete the second sentence so that it has a similar meaning to the first sentence. Use the correct active or passive form of the verbs in brackets.

1 Extra homework is given to the students every day.
The students _____. (give)
2 His books aren't sold in the USA.
Bookshops in the USA _____. (not sell)
3 The library was destroyed in an earthquake.
An earthquake _____. (destroy)
4 The children didn't break the window.
The window _____. (not break)
5 Hundreds of products use plastic.
Plastic _____. (use/in)
6 The thief was caught by the police.
The police _____. (catch)
7 No one told us about the exam.
We _____. (not tell)
8 You don't find tigers in Africa.
Tigers _____. (not find)

LISTENING

6 A ▶ 10.3 Read the text and look at the pictures. What issues do you think each person will talk about? Listen and check.

WE ASKED PEOPLE FROM DIFFERENT GENERATIONS THREE QUESTIONS:

1 What annoys you about modern life?

2 How can we stop it?

3 What punishments do you propose?

We asked a sixteen-year-old, a thirty-five-year-old and a seventy-year-old. You may find their answers surprising. Or maybe not!

A

B

C

B Listen again and choose the correct options.

1 Sophie
  a) is a teacher.
  b) works with technology.
  c) is a schoolgirl.

2 Sophie thinks people concentrate better
  a) when they use technology.
  b) without technology.
  c) when they wear headphones.

3 Luis doesn't like
  a) newspapers and food in the tube.
  b) food at work.
  c) the government.

4 What punishment does Luis suggest?
  a) cleaning the tube
  b) paying some money
  c) cleaning the streets

5 Pamela loves
  a) her older friends.
  b) being old.
  c) technology.

6 What punishment does Pamela suggest?
  a) reading emails from her
  b) writing spam messages
  c) reading spam messages

7 Read the sentences and find words that match the meanings.

1 'They spend their whole life wearing headphones. I think it's really rude.'
not polite: _____

2 'In my school they banned personal technology during lessons.'
formally said that people must not do something:
_____

3 'For me, the worst thing is litter on the street.'
unwanted paper, bottles, etc. that people leave in a public place: _____

4 'People just leave their newspapers lying around.'
when something is left somewhere, in the wrong place: _____

5 'All this paper is a real mess.'
untidy, with everything in the wrong place:
_____

6 'The government has tried to introduce fines, but it hasn't worked.'
money you have to pay as a punishment:
_____

7 'Spam is so annoying.'
making you feel angry: _____

VOCABULARY
PROBLEMS

1 Read the clues and complete the crossword.

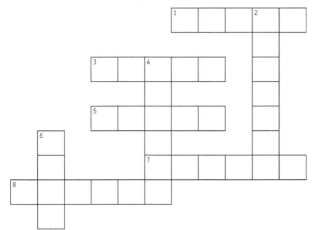

Across
1 when a computer suddenly stops working
3 when you have to wait for something because it's late
5 when you can't move, e.g. in traffic or a small place
7 paper, cans, bottles, etc. that people do not want and leave in public places
8 not working properly (e.g. for equipment)

Down
2 help that is given to you in a restaurant or shop
4 when people speak like this on their phone in a public place, it can be very annoying
6 unwanted emails that advertise something

FUNCTION
COMPLAINING

2 Choose the correct options to complete the conversation.

A: Hello. Can I help at all?
B: Yes, there's a ¹_____ the television in my room.
A: What exactly is the problem?
B: It ²_____.
A: OK. I'll ³_____ it right away. Is there anything else I can help you with?
B: Yes. I ordered room service this morning but I had to wait ⁴_____ an hour.
A: I'm really ⁵_____ that, sir.
B: And my room was very noisy last night.
A: I'm afraid there's nothing we can ⁶_____ that, sir. There's a disco downstairs.
B: Every night?
A: Oh no, sir. On Mondays there's a rock concert.

1 a) problem with   b) problem for   c) big problem
2 a) isn't work   b) not work   c) doesn't work
3 a) check into   b) look into   c) look up
4 a) at over   b) for above   c) for over
5 a) sorry for   b) sorry about   c) very sorry
6 a) make about   b) do for   c) do about

3 A Look at the pictures and write sentences using the prompts.

1 there / problem / printer
_____

2 microphone / not work
_____

3 been / here / over two hours
_____

B Match responses a)–c) with complaints 1–3 in Exercise 3A.

a) I'm really sorry about that. I was stuck in a traffic jam.   _____
b) I'll look into it right away. For now, you can use the printer on the second floor.   _____
c) I'm sorry but there's nothing we can do at the moment. We don't have any electricity.   _____

LEARN TO
SOUND FIRM, BUT POLITE

4 A Complete the sentences with a word that matches the stress pattern in brackets.

1 Sorry, but there's a ___problem___ with my room. (Oo)
2 _____ me. I've been here for over an hour. (oO)
3 _____ I speak to the manager? I'm not happy with the service. (O)
4 Could you _____ me? There's something wrong with this computer. (O)
5 I'm _____ I have a problem. The air conditioner in my room doesn't work. (oO)
6 I have to make a _____. The waitress was rude to me. (oO)

B ▶ 10.4 Listen and check. Then listen and repeat. Focus on the stressed words in the sentences.

TECHNOLOGY

VOCABULARY
COMMUNICATION

1 Complete the sentences with the words in the box.

| email webpage Skype mobile post blog |
| chat link video send |

1 Do you mind if I use your _____ phone?
2 I've just started writing a new _____ where I write about politics, and lots of people are reading it.
3 Have you seen that video with the cat? Wait, I'll share the _____ so you can see it.
4 I'm just going to check my _____ for new messages.
5 Why don't you _____ her an SMS?
6 If you're at home later, I'll _____ you so we can talk about the plans for the weekend.
7 Have you updated the _____ with our new photos?
8 We don't see each other often, but we _____ a lot online.
9 I've lost my phone, so I'm going to _____ a message online asking people to send me their numbers.
10 I love filming birds in the park. I usually edit the movies, then upload them to a _____ sharing site.

GRAMMAR
PRESENT PERFECT

2 Put the words in the correct order to complete the conversations.

1 **A:** Are you ready for your holiday?
  B: packing / I / finished / yet / haven't
  _____

2 **A:** Don't forget to call Amy.
  B: already / to / I've / her / spoken
  _____

3 **A:** Hi. You look well!
  B: just / from / we've / holiday / back / yes, / got / our
  _____

4 **A:** Is that the new *Shining Stars* DVD?
  B: haven't / yet / it / watched / yes, / I / but
  _____

5 **A:** my / results / just / exam / got / I've
  B: Tell me! How did you do?
  _____

6 **A:** You need to buy a present for Josh.
  B: money / but / already / all / I've / spent / my
  _____

3 Complete the sentences. Use *just* and the present perfect form of the verbs in brackets.

1 I'm still tired. I _____ (wake up).
2 Well done. You _____ (finish) all your work for today.
3 I don't want any lunch, thanks. I _____ (eat).
4 I don't believe it. Sam _____ (lose) his phone again!
5 That's brilliant! Helen _____ (pass) her driving test.
6 I'm really sorry. I _____ (hear) the bad news.
7 Hold on a minute, I'll check. Sheila _____ (send) me a message.
8 Let's go for a walk. It _____ (stop) raining.
9 Hurry up! The taxi _____ (arrive).
10 You're a bit late. They _____ (start) the meeting.

4 A Complete the conversations using the prompts.

1 **A:** *Have you finished the book yet* ?
     (you / finish / book / yet)
  B: Yes, I've already started the next one.

2 **A:** _____ ?
     (you / cook / dinner / yet)
  B: No, _____ .
     (I / only / just / get home)

3 **A:** _____ ?
     (you ask / wife / yet)
  B: No, I'm going to speak to her later.

4 **A:** _____ ?
     (you / decided / where / we're going / yet)
  B: Yes, _____ .
     (we / just / book / a table / Mario's)

5 **A:** Do you want to come and play football?
  B: No, _____ .
     (I / already / play / twice / this week)

6 **A:** _____ ?
     (you / see / Miranda)
  B: Yes, _____ .
     (she / just / leave)

B ▶ 11.1 Listen and check.

READING

5 Read the text and choose the best title.

a) The oldest blogger in the world hated the internet

b) Spain's blogging granny was a huge a success

c) Spanish granny used pen and paper

1 'No one listens to old people,' says Maria Amelia López on her blog. But she was wrong. A lot of people listened to her. When she died, aged ninety-seven, López was thought to be the world's oldest blogger and  she was certainly one of the most successful. Her first post was made on her ninety-fifth birthday. It read, 'Today it's my birthday and my grandson, who is very stingy, gave me a blog.'

2 A later post reads, 'Since that day I've had 1,570,784 visits from bloggers from five continents who have cheered up my old age.' From cleaning ladies in Brazil to the Spanish president, people have enjoyed reading what López had to say. She was funny and friendly and she had some strong opinions. 'Old people need to wake up a bit,' she said. 'You have to live life. Don't take pills and fall asleep in the armchair.'

3 At first, López didn't know anything about computers. 'I thought a blog was a kind of paper notebook,' she said. But her grandson, Daniel, who she lived with, set up a blog for her as a birthday present. At the time he had no idea how it would change their lives. López received hundreds of emails, many in languages she didn't understand. Although she had other helpers, including Daniel, and friends she met on the internet, she couldn't reply to everyone.

4 When she was on her own, López loved reading the online newspapers and chatting on the internet. She said it helped her to keep in touch with the younger generation. Teenagers wrote to López to tell her about their lives and ask her for advice. She thought that everybody should use the internet. For López, it was one of the best experiences of her life.

6 Read the text again. Are the statements true (T) or false (F)?

1 People from all around the world have read Maria López's blog. _____

2 López knew a lot about computers before she started writing the blog. _____

3 López's grandson started the blog for her a birthday present. _____

4 He knew that the internet would change López's life. _____

5 López always replied to the emails she received. _____

6 The internet put López in touch with younger people. _____

7 Find words in the text that match these meanings.

1 a message on a website/blog (paragraph 1)

_____

2 not generous; not wanting to spend money (paragraph 1)

_____

3 people who read/write a blog (paragraph 2)

_____

4 ideas you believe in strongly (paragraph 2)

_____

5 started (paragraph 3)

_____

6 all the people of about the same age (paragraph 4)

_____

WRITING

PRONOUNS

8 Rewrite the second sentence in each pair using the pronouns in the box.

it here us ~~there~~ her them

1 We went to the beach. We had a lovely
   there
   time ⌄ ~~on the beach~~.

2 I visited my grandmother. I took my grandmother out to lunch.

3 I'm seeing some friends. I haven't seen my friends for a long time.

4 He's just started a new job. He's enjoying the new job.

5 The waiter smiled at Mark and me. Then he gave Mark and me the bill.

6 This place is so beautiful. I'd like to stay in this place for ever.

VOCABULARY
FEELINGS

1 How would you feel in these situations? Match the situations with the words in the box.

> uncomfortable   bored   nervous   lonely   confused
> worried   amazed   excited

1 It's your birthday and you're having a party.

_____

2 You've just bought a new computer and you are trying to read the instructions.

_____

3 You're standing on a crowded train, carrying heavy bags, and you're hot.

_____

4 You have to give a talk to 300 people.

_____

5 You've decided to spend a year in another country, but you haven't met any friends yet.

_____

6 You've got a bad cough and you've had it for more than six months.

_____

7 You're waiting at a station and your train has been delayed for two hours.

_____

8 You're waiting in an airport and you see a friend who you haven't seen for ten years.

_____

2 ▶ 11.2 Listen to six people talking about feelings. Match the feeling each speaker talks about 1–6 with the things he/she says about it a)–f).

1	bored	a)	anything to do with numbers
2	lonely	b)	prefers to be busy
3	confused	c)	the beauty of nature
4	amazed	d)	problems of the world
5	nervous	e)	call a friend/sister
6	worried	f)	organise a party/dinner

GRAMMAR
REAL CONDITIONALS + WHEN

3 Match the sentence halves.

1 We'll go for a walk   _____
2 If she passes her exams,   _____
3 We'll be there to meet you at the airport   _____
4 I'm sure he'll make lots of new friends   _____
5 If you like the music,   _____
6 If you're very busy now,   _____
7 They'll hear us coming in   _____
8 If you plan your talk carefully,   _____

a) I'll get you a CD.
b) if we make too much noise.
c) when the plane arrives.
d) if the weather gets better.
e) you'll be fine.
f) she'll go to university.
g) I'll come back later.
h) when he starts his course.

4 Complete the sentences with the correct form of the verbs in brackets.

1 If I _____ (be) late again, my girlfriend _____ (be) furious!

2 I _____ (call) you if there _____ (be) a problem.

3 When I _____ (see) Mary, I _____ (tell) her you were here.

4 If the taxi _____ (not come) soon, we _____ (be) late.

5 If I _____ (get) another job, I _____ (earn) a bit more money.

6 I _____ (buy) you some lunch if you _____ (be) hungry.

7 They _____ (change) their minds when they _____ (see) the hotel.

8 What _____ (you/do) if you _____ (lose) your job?

5 Complete the conversation with the correct form of the verbs in the box.

> stay   wait   not know   have (x2)   spend   find
> go (x2)   be   look (x2)

A: We need to book our summer holiday. If we
¹_____ any longer, everything ²_____
fully booked.

B: You're right. But we still haven't decided where to go.

A: How about Spain?

B: If we ³_____ to Spain, I'm sure we
⁴_____ good weather. But we always go to
Spain.

A: Paris?

B: We could try, but if we ⁵_____ in Paris, we
⁶_____ lots of money. Paris is really expensive.

A: OK. How about Romania or Bulgaria?

B: We could try that. But if we ⁷_____ there, we
⁸_____ the language.

A: That doesn't matter.

B: I know, and if we ⁹_____ on the internet, we
might ¹⁰_____ some cheap deals.

A: That's a good idea. If you ¹¹_____ time later,
¹²_____ (you)?

B: OK. But I'm not going to Paris. I don't have enough
money!

6 Look at the picture and write sentences using the prompts.

1 when the man / cross / bridge / he / give /
his girlfriend / flowers
When the man crosses the bridge, he will give his
girlfriend the flowers.

2 if / elephant / walk on bridge / the bridge / break
_____

3 if / bridge / break / the elephant / fall.
_____

4 if / elephant / fall / the crocodiles / eat it
_____

5 if / man / fall / girlfriend / scream
_____

6 if / girlfriend / scream / snake / wake up
_____

7 if / snake / wake up / bite / girlfriend
_____

8 if / man / not cross / bridge / can keep / flowers
_____

9 if / he / keep / flowers / it / be / a lot easier
_____

LISTENING

7 ▶ 11.3 Listen to two people answering the question
below. Circle the correct answers to the questions in
the table.

Are new computer games changing the way we live?

		Robert	Miriam
1	Does he/she think computer games are changing the way we live?	yes / no	yes / no
2	Does he/she use a computer for work?	yes / no	yes / no
3	Does he/she enjoy computer games?	yes / no	yes / no
4	Does he/she play a lot?	yes / no	yes / no

8 A Complete Robert and Miriam's statements.

Robert

1 I think they've already _____
the way we live.

2 This has made me a more
_____ person.

3 I spend most of my free time talking to other people
with the same _____.

4 These days I find it easier to
_____ to people I don't know.

Miriam

5 There are lots of games I don't like, like the
_____ games.

6 I don't spend all my time on the
_____.

7 And I think a lot of people are like
_____.

8 In our free time we _____ to
do other things.

B ▶ 11.3 Listen again and check.

VOCABULARY
INTERNET TERMS

1 Complete the words in the sentences.

1 I use Google a lot, but I use other s_ _rch _ng_n_s too.

2 Sometimes I read the discussions on the m_ss_g_ b_ _rds. It's interesting to see what other people think about things.

3 I don't use any of the s_c_ _l n_tw_ _k_ng sites because I just don't have time. I prefer to talk to friends on the phone or send them an email.

4 I look at tr_v_l w_bs_t_s when I'm planning a holiday. It's useful to get ideas of where you could go.

5 I read a few different _nl_n_ n_ws sites because I like reading news from other countries.

6 I get all my music from m_s_c d_wnl_ _d sites.

7 When I've got a few minutes to spare, I look at the ph_t_ sh_r_ng sites and find interesting pictures.

FUNCTION
GIVING OPINIONS

2 Complete the conversations with the words in the box.

my   true   don't   definitely   that's   sure   totally

1 **A:** It's always better to do your shopping online.
  B: I _____ think that's true. It's not always cheaper.

2 **A:** People who live in rich countries should give money to people in poorer countries.
  B: In _____ opinion, that's not the best way to solve the problem.

3 **A:** This bar is much nicer than the one we came to last time.
  B: _____. I really like it here.

4 **A:** If you want people to work harder, you need to pay them more money.
  B: _____ right.

5 **A:** I think our product is the best on the market.
  B: I'm not _____ about that.

6 **A:** You need to control how many people move into the country.
  B: I _____ disagree. I think people should be allowed to live where they want.

7 **A:** Not everyone has a mobile phone, even nowadays.
  B: That's _____, although most people do.

LEARN TO
DISAGREE POLITELY

3 Put the words in the correct order to make polite responses.

1 don't / I / sorry, / think / right / I'm / but / that's
_____

2 disagree / totally / I'm / I / afraid.
_____

3 not / about / I'm / sure / that / really
_____

4 sorry, / don't / so / I'm / think / I / but
_____

4 A Read the conversation. Change the responses in brackets to make them more polite.

Manager: The project needs to be finished this week.
Worker: ¹_____. (That's not possible.)
Manager: Why not? Everything's possible.
Worker: ²_____. (I don't think it is.) We're working hard, but we need another two weeks to finish the job.
Manager: Two weeks? Can you try to finish by the end of next week?
Worker: ³_____ (I'm not sure.) There's still a lot of work to do.
Manager: That's true. But you can get some more staff so we can finish sooner.
⁴_____. (I don't see what the problem is.)
Worker: ⁵_____. (I disagree.) The problem is that we don't have more staff. We can't find people to start work tomorrow, so …

B ▶ 11.4 Listen and check.

C ▶ 11.5 Listen and repeat. Copy the polite intonation.

VOCABULARY

FILM

1 Match the types of film in the box with the descriptions.

action film   comedy   blockbuster   science fiction film   biopic
~~historical drama~~   horror film   thriller   cartoon   documentary

1 It tells a story from many years ago. ___historical drama___
2 It is animated with pictures. _____
3 It is funny. _____
4 It tells the story of someone's life. _____
5 It shows something true or real and doesn't usually have actors. _____
6 It is frightening. _____
7 It has lots of fights, guns and explosions. _____
8 It might show people from another planet or technology of the future. _____
9 It is very successful. _____
10 It is exciting because you don't know what will happen in the end. _____

GRAMMAR

REPORTED SPEECH

2 Tick (✓) the correct sentences. Cross (✗) the incorrect sentences.

1 a) Sandra told us she would be here at 6.00.   ✓
  b) Sandra said us she would be here at 6.00.   ✗
2 a) He said me he wanted to be a lawyer.
  b) He told me he wanted to be a lawyer.
3 a) I bought orange juice because you said you didn't like apple juice.
  b) I bought orange juice because you told you didn't like apple juice.
4 a) The doctor said them he couldn't cure the illness.
  b) The doctor told them he couldn't cure the illness.
5 a) Mary told to us she was writing the great American novel.
  b) Mary said she was writing the great American novel.
6 a) Luca and Giselle said us their plane would arrive at 9.30.
  b) Luca and Giselle told us their plane would arrive at 9.30.

3 Match the sentence halves.

1 John was cooking steak, so I told him ____
2 Dave asked if we liked the theatre, but I told him ____
3 I called Reuben on his mobile, but he said ____
4 Maisie invited me to dinner, so I said ____
5 We invited him to work with us, but he said ____
6 I asked her if she felt OK and she told me ____
7 They asked if it was a boy or a girl, so I said ____
8 I needed help with my algebra homework, but Dad said ____
9 Jim asked about her tennis, but she told him ____
10 Our neighbour wanted a map of London, but I told her ____

a) we wouldn't know until June.
b) he couldn't do maths.
c) we preferred the cinema.
d) she wasn't playing any more.
e) he was working for another company.
f) we didn't have one.
g) I'd see if I was free tonight.
h) I didn't eat meat.
i) she always felt tired in the afternoon.
j) he couldn't hear me.

4 Report what Bill said.

1 'I'm an actor.'
  He said ___he was an actor___.
2 'I'm starring in a TV series.'
  He told me _____.
3 'I'll appear in a film next year.'
  He said _____.
4 'The film is called Samba Nights.'
  He told me _____.
5 'I can work with any Hollywood directors I choose.'
  He said _____.
6 'I'm living in Beverly Hills.'
  He told me _____.
7 'I'm getting married to Sonia Jeffers next month.'
  He said _____.
8 'She is a famous actor, too.'
  He told me _____.
9 'I'll text you next week.'
  He said _____.
10 'I can take you to some great parties.'
  He told me _____.

LISTENING

5 A Match the famous lines from films 1–5 to actors A–E. Do you know which film each line is from?

1 'ET phone home.'
(film: _____)

2 'I'll be back.'
(film: _____)

3 'You talking to me?'
(film: _____)

4 'My name's Bond. James Bond.'
(film: _____)

5 'Frankly, my dear, I don't give a damn.'
(film: _____)

A

Robert De Niro

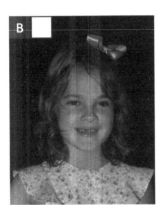

B

Drew Barrymore

C

Clark Gable

D

Arnold Schwarzenegger

E

Sean Connery

B ▶ 12.1 Listen and check.

C Listen again and answer the questions.

1 How old was Drew Barrymore when she played Gertie?
2 How does the Terminator get into the police station when he returns?
3 Who came up with the line 'You talking to me?'
4 When did Sean Connery first say the famous James Bond line?
5 What was shocking about the famous line from *Gone with the Wind*?

D Match the words in bold in sentences 1–5 with dictionary definitions a)–e).

1 One of these is the **line**, 'ET phone home.'. _____
2 It made her one of the biggest child **stars** of the time. _____
3 In a **scene** in *The Terminator* in 1984, Arnold Schwarzenegger tries to get into a police station, but they don't let him in. _____
4 Sometimes words are connected to the **role**, not the actor who says them. _____
5 This was perhaps the most famous line ever said **on screen**. _____

a) | *n, [C]* a character in a play or film

b) | *n, [C]* a famous actor, singer, sports player, etc.

c) | *n, [C]* a character in a play or film

d) | *n, [C]* a sentence which someone says in a play or film

e) | *prep+n* during a film or a television programme

E Complete an actor's post with words from Exercise 5D. Change the form if necessary.

Jack Jones

Just found out I'm going to be in a
¹ _____ in this film with Emily Sharp!
She's my hero! I've seen her ² _____
lots of times and she's always brilliant. She's
going to be a big ³ _____. She has the
biggest ⁴ _____ in the film – she plays
a reporter who discovers a city under the
Earth. I have two ⁵ _____ to say where
I ask her a question and then say how I feel.
I can't wait!

VOCABULARY
SUFFIXES

1 Complete the words with suffixes.

1 The guide contains lots of use_ful_ information.
2 He's quite famous now. He's been very success_____ in his career.
3 We've been married for forty years! We're having a celebrat_____.
4 You spent a week in the jungle? How adventur_____ of you!
5 Don't believe what that politic_____ says. He just wants you to vote for him.
6 We've asked a professional photograph_____ to take the photos.
7 It's been a wonder_____ holiday. Thank you so much.
8 I never ride motorbikes. They're too danger_____.
9 Thank you so much. You've been very help_____.

2 A Write the words in the correct column for each stress pattern.

> adventurous   politician   wonderful   musician
> celebrity   scientist   invention

1 ooOo	2 oOoo	3 oOo	4 Ooo
celebration	photographer	successful	dangerous

B ▶ **12.2** Listen and check. Then listen and repeat.

GRAMMAR
HYPOTHETICAL CONDITIONALS

3 Complete the hypothetical conditional sentences with the correct form of the verbs in brackets.

1 If he _____ (not have) a lot of money, she _____ (not be) interested in him.
2 If I _____ (not have) an exam tomorrow, I _____ (love) to come out with you.
3 We _____ (be) so much happier if we _____ (not argue) all the time.
4 I'm sure she _____ (ask) you if she _____ (need) some help.
5 If it _____ (not rain) so much, we _____ (go out) more often.
6 You _____ (not be) so tired if you _____ (go) to bed earlier.
7 If I _____ (have) my car here, I _____ (offer) to drive you home.
8 If he _____ (can) find a job there, he _____ (move) to Spain.

4 Write sentences using the prompts.

1 if I / be / famous / people / recognise / me on the street
_____
2 if she / have / more money / she / buy / a car
_____
3 what / you / do / if you / lose / your job?
_____
4 if I / lose / my job / I / have to / look for another one
_____
5 I / travel / to China / if I / can / speak Mandarin
_____
6 if Harry / have / more time / he / do / more sport
_____
7 if we / not have / a television / I / read / more books
_____
8 if you / be / famous / how / your life / change?
_____

5 Rewrite the sentences using hypothetical conditionals.

1 I'm very tired, so I'm not going out later.
If I wasn't so tired, I would go out later.
2 The restaurant is very expensive, so we don't eat there.
_____
3 You don't water the garden, so it doesn't look very good.
_____
4 I don't have Jodie's number, so I can't call her.
_____
5 We don't have enough money, so we can't buy our own house.
_____
6 I don't have any food in the house, so I won't invite them in for lunch.
_____
7 I don't practise every day, so I'm not very good at the guitar.
_____
8 I spend so much time answering my email that I don't finish my other work.
_____
9 The flights are expensive so we don't visit very often.
_____
10 I'm very late, so I'm walking quickly.
_____

READING

6 Read the text and complete the summary with one or two words in each gap.

The biggest music video ever

1 On 21 December 2012, *Gangnam Style*, a music video by Korean musician Psy, became the first video in internet history to be watched by a billion people. This was such a high number that YouTube had to update its software to work with so many visitors. In May 2014, YouTube said that the video had two billion views – another world record.

2 The song is about Seoul's fashionable Gangnam area (often compared to Beverly Hills in California), and laughs at people who try to appear high class by saying they are 'Gangnam Style'. Psy laughs at them by singing *oppan Gangnam style*, saying he is 'Gangnam style' too.

3 The song has a unique dance, called the Horse Trot, where Psy dances like he is riding a horse. He said it took him a month to invent the dance, working with a professional dancer every day. They also tried moving like a panda and a kangaroo. Even important people such as Barack Obama and David Cameron have tried the dance, with mixed results. And in 2012 UN Secretary-General Ban Ki-moon said it was something which could create peace in the world!

4 The song was hugely successful. The South Korean government said that in 2012 it brought $13.4 million into the country. People in the music industry said it helped develop the internet as a way of making music popular. This means that music can come from anywhere, not just from North America and Europe. Love it or hate it, everyone knows the song. Just don't listen to it first thing in the morning, or you'll be singing it all day!

Gangnam Style is a ¹ _music video_ which has had over two ² _____ views. The song is about the Gangnam area in ³ _____, South Korea, and the people who go there. There is a ⁴ _____ which goes with the song, called the Horse Trot. It took Psy a month to create. Many ⁵ _____ have also tried the dance. The song has been very successful and helped bring a lot of ⁶ _____ into the South Korean economy. It has also helped change the world's ⁷ _____ industry.

---

7 Read the text again. Are the sentences true (T) or false (F)?

1 The video reached two billion views in 2012. _____
2 The song makes a joke about people in the Gangnam area. _____
3 Psy thinks he is really 'Gangnam Style'. _____
4 The Gangnam Style dance tries to copy a panda and a kangaroo. _____
5 Ban Ki-moon thought the song was a good thing for the world. _____
6 *Gangnam Style* is a difficult song to forget. _____

8 Find words or expressions in the text to match these meanings.

1 change something to make it better/more modern (paragraph 1) _____
2 popular at a particular time (paragraph 2) _____
3 the only one of its kind (paragraph 3) _____
4 make something happen or exist (paragraph 3) _____
5 extremely (paragraph 4) _____

WRITING

PARAGRAPHS

9 A Put the sentences in the correct order under the headings to form three paragraphs.

Introduction/Early life
_b_ , ___, ___, ___,

Career
___, ___, ___, ___, ___,

Personal life
___, ___, ___,

a) During the 70s and 80s Clint starred in many successful films, but it wasn't until 1990 that he won an Oscar for Best Director and a nomination for Best Actor, for his role in *Unforgiven* (1992).

b) Clint Eastwood is perhaps one of the most famous international film stars of the twentieth century.

c) Although he started, he never finished his college degree in business studies.

d) He has been married twice and also had a long-term relationship with his co-star Sondra Locke.

e) All three films were hits, particularly the third, and Eastwood became an instant international star.

f) Eastwood has seven children, from five different women.

g) Instead, he found work as an actor in B-movies and later in a well-known television programme.

h) In December 2014, after eighteen years together, he and his second wife, Dina Ruiz, divorced.

i) Born in 1930, in San Francisco, Clint Eastwood was the son of a steel worker.

j) After this success, he was given excellent roles in films like *Where Eagles Dare*, in which he starred with Richard Burton.

k) Around this time, he also started to direct films, as well as act in them.

l) In the 1960s, Clint was given important roles in western films *A Fistful of Dollars* (1964), *For a Few Dollars More* (1965) and later *The Good, the Bad and the Ugly* (1966).

B Write your own biography (or invent one) using the headings in Exercise 9A (100–150 words).

VOCABULARY
COLLOCATIONS

1 Underline the correct alternatives.

TravelBig
What our customers say about us

We paid a lot for our holiday with TravelBig, but it was definitely worth it. Lena, our guide, did so many things for us! On the first night there was a concert we wanted to go to and she ¹*took/did/got* tickets for us. On the second day we ²*worked/rented/invited* a car and drove around the nearby towns. She ³*offered/ requested/recommended* a great place – the old ruins just outside the town – and she even ⁴*organised/ made/paid* a private tour for us! On our final night we ⁵*helped/offered/invited* Lena to dinner and she ⁶*bought/booked/rented* a table in one of the best restaurants I have ever been to. I would definitely recommend TravelBig.

Pablo Gonzalez

FUNCTION
REQUESTS AND OFFERS

2 Match the sentence halves.

1 I'd	a) get me a ticket for the concert?
2 Would it be	b) table for four?
3 Would you be able to	c) to ask for a better seat?
4 Could you recommend	d) possible to invite my cousin?
5 Shall I book a	e) you like me to call a taxi?
6 Do you want me	f) a good dentist?
7 Would	g) like to rent a boat for six people.

3 Complete the sentences with the phrases in the box.

> you recommend   would like   like me
> be possible   want me   shall I   able to

1 They _____ a holiday in a hot country.
2 Would it _____ to rent a car at the airport?
3 Would you be _____ get me a ticket?
4 Could _____ a good doctor?
5 _____ speak to your teacher about the problem?
6 Do you _____ to take that bag for you?
7 Would you _____ to find a good restaurant?

LEARN TO
ASK FOR MORE TIME

4 Underline the correct alternatives.
  1 **A:** Would it be possible to get an appointment with Dr Jones?
    B: Can you *get/give* me a moment? I'll see if he has any time this week.
  2 **A:** Do you have Paula's phone number?
    B: Hang *on/off*. I don't know where I put my mobile.
  3 **A:** Is this a good time to discuss the agenda for the meeting?
    B: Just *the/a* moment. There's another caller on the line.
  4 **A:** Johnny! Open the door!
    B: Hold *in/on*! I'm in the shower!

LISTENING

5 A **12.3 Listen and match pictures A–C with conversations 1–3.**

A

B

C

B Listen again and complete the table.

	1	2	3
1 What do the customers want?			
2 Do they get what they want?			

GRAMMAR USES OF *LIKE*

1 Complete the conversations using the prompts in brackets. Use phrases with *like*.

  1 A: What kind of music _do you like_?
     (you)

    B: I like all kinds of things – indie, hard rock and dance.

  2 A: Is that the new John Grisham book? _____? (what)

    B: It's great. I can't put it down.

  3 A: _____ eating out in restaurants? (you)

    B: Not really. I prefer to go to someone's house for dinner.

  4 A: I haven't met Amélie's new boyfriend yet. _____? (he)

    B: He's really nice. And he's handsome too.

  5 A: Do you get on well with your sister? _____ doing the same things? (you)

    B: Yes, we do. We're both very sociable. We like going out to parties.

  6 A: Is it cold there today? _____? (what/weather)

    B: No, it's not cold at all. The sun's shining.

VOCABULARY DESCRIBING A CITY

2 Complete the sentences with the words in the box.

buildings	pollution	crime	safe
nightlife	polite	transport	traffic

  1 It's a very _____ area. There's hardly any crime at all.

  2 There are a lot of factories around the city, so the _____ is quite bad.

  3 I try to use public _____, so I get the bus or take the train.

  4 It's a bad time of day to go by car. There's so much _____.

  5 There are parties most nights and good clubs to go to. The _____ is great.

  6 I love the cities in Italy. They have so many beautiful _____.

  7 People in the shops are friendly and _____. They smile and say 'Good morning'.

  8 The _____ in the area is much worse nowadays. It's dangerous to walk alone at night.

GRAMMAR PRESENT/PAST PASSIVE

3 Underline the correct alternatives.

> Over $7,500 [1]*finds/was found* in a shoe box by a lady who [2]*works/is worked* in a charity shop in the USA. Teodora Petrova, who recently [3]*arrived/was arrived* from Bulgaria, [4]*found/was found* the money on her first day at work at the shop. The money [5]*was hidden/hid* inside a pair of shoes. When Teodora made the discovery, she immediately [6]*gave/was given* the money to her manager. The charity bosses [7]*told/were told* what happened and they have said that they are looking for the person who [8]*gave/was given* the shoes to the shop, as they probably [9]*left/was left* the money inside by accident. If the owner of the money [10]*is not found/does not find*, the money will be kept by the charity.

VOCABULARY CRIME AND PUNISHMENT

4 Complete the words in the sentences.

  1 Statistics show that short prison s_nt_nc_s are not as effective as community s__rv__c__ in stopping crimes.

  2 The police took my car away and I had to pay a f__n__.

  3 People who shop online can easily become victims of fr__ __d.

  4 An old man stopped the th__ __f as he tried to run away from the bank.

  5 He always drives too fast, so he was stopped for sp__ __d__ng.

  6 The sides of the trains are always covered in gr__ff__t__.

GRAMMAR PRESENT PERFECT

5 Complete the conversations with the present perfect form of the verbs in brackets.

  1 A: Have you seen my files anywhere?
    B: Yes, I_'ve just put_ (just/put) them on your desk.

  2 A: Have you put the rubbish out yet?
    B: Yes, I _____ (just/do) it.

  3 A: Have you started the project?
    B: Yes, but I _____ (not finish/yet).

  4 A: Do we need to pay the electrician?
    B: No, I _____ (already/pay) him.

  5 A: Have you finished your work yet?
    B: No, I _____ (just/start)!

  6 A: Has the post arrived yet?
    B: Yes, the postman _____ (just/bring) it.

VOCABULARY INTERNET TERMS, PROBLEMS

6 Put the letters in the correct order to complete the sentences.

  1 I can't stand it! That's the third time my computer has _____ (desrach) this morning.

  2 The printer doesn't work. I think it's _____ (yaflut).

  3 I'll send an _____ (MSS) to his phone.

  4 I'll book our tickets on that travel _____ (twiesbe).

  5 I didn't know anything about it, so I looked on one of the _____ (shecra) engines.

  6 I can't stand it when people speak _____ (lldoyu) on their phones. It's really annoying.

  7 Did you read Jake's post on that message _____ (bdora)?

GRAMMAR REAL AND HYPOTHETICAL CONDITIONALS

7 Underline the correct alternatives.

1 If I were you, I *will/would* talk to him about the problem.
2 If the traffic is bad, I *will/would* be late.
3 If I *know/knew* the answer, I would tell you.
4 You *will/would* miss the train if you don't hurry up.
5 If I *am/was* the president, I would change the law.
6 If he works hard, he *will/would* get a pay rise.
7 I'm sure they'll have children if they *get/got* married.
8 If we *leave/left* the country, my mother wouldn't be very happy.

VOCABULARY FEELINGS

8 Circle the correct option to complete the sentences.

1 There's nothing to do here except lie on the beach. I'm really _____.
   a) confused   b) bored
2 She spends a lot of time on her own. I think she's very _____.
   a) excited   b) lonely
3 I didn't know anyone at the party, so I felt a little _____.
   a) uncomfortable   b) amazed
4 I've got an interview for a new job tomorrow and I'm really _____.
   a) nervous   b) bored
5 Everybody is telling me to do different things. I'm really _____.
   a) lonely   b) confused.
6 Paolo's not answering his phone. I'm _____ that something has happened to him.
   a) confused   b) worried

VOCABULARY SUFFIXES

9 Add suffixes to the words in the box to complete the sentences.

politic   ~~danger~~   photograph   wonder   help   success

1 Why do you drive so fast? It's ___*dangerous*___ .
2 He's a very _____ actor. Now he's a millionaire.
3 I studied politics at university, but I decided not to become a _____.
4 We told the receptionist about the problem, and she was really _____.
5 It was a _____ evening. I enjoyed it very much.
6 I've always enjoyed taking photos. I've been a professional _____ for about ten years now.

GRAMMAR REPORTED SPEECH

10 Find and correct the mistakes in the sentences.

1 Suzie told to me that they wanted to move house.
2 We said her that we wouldn't be long.
3 I called a taxi, but they told they were busy.
4 They asked to move to a different table, but the waitress said them that it wasn't possible.
5 Her boss told to her that she had to work late.

VOCABULARY FILM

11 Complete the sentences with types of film.

1 I watched a really good ___*biopic*___ about Winston Churchill's life last night.
2 It's a brilliant _____. I laughed so much!
3 I can't watch _____ films. I'm too scared.
4 It's an _____ film, with a lot of car chases.
5 *Atonement* is a _____ drama about WWII.
6 I don't like _____ films about aliens coming from outer space.

FUNCTION REVISION

12 A Complete the conversations with the phrases in the boxes.

> there's a problem   I'm sorry about that
> could you help

1 **A:** Excuse me, _____ me?
  B: Yes, of course. What can I do?
  A: _____ with my key. It doesn't open the door.
  B: _____. I'll get you another one.

> there's nothing we can do   I'm afraid I have
> excuse me, could I speak to

2 **A:** _____ the manager?
  B: Yes. I'll just get him for you.
  A: _____ a complaint.
  C: What seems to be the problem?
  A: We still haven't had our main course.
  C: I'm sorry, but _____ at the moment. We're very busy.

> certainly   would you like me to   no problem
> could you recommend

3 **A:** _____ a good place to go shopping?
  B: _____. There's a new shopping centre not far from here. _____ order you a taxi?
  A: That would be great. Thank you.
  B: _____.

B ▶ R4.1 Listen and check.

CHECK

Circle the correct option to complete the sentences.

1 I haven't met the boss yet. _____ she like?
   a) What is   b) What has   c) How is
2 So you're enjoying life in Argentina. What _____ like about it?
   a) are you   b) is it   c) do you
3 The toys _____ here, not in Japan.
   a) are made   b) are making   c) have made
4 Everyone in the hotel _____ by the police. They still don't know who did it.
   a) interviewed   b) was interviewed
   c) has interviewed
5 People _____ to prison when they commit a crime.
   a) send   b) were sent   c) are sent
6 The internet connection doesn't _____.
   a) fix   b) on   c) work
7 We'll look into it _____ away.
   a) right   b) for   c) go
8 Why is everyone talking so _____?
   a) loud   b) loudly   c) noisy
9 There were terrible _____ at the airport.
   a) litter   b) delays   c) service
10 There are so many people at the party. The room is very _____.
   a) crowded   b) empty   c) safe
11 Why do you keep calling him? You've _____ called him three times this morning!
   a) just   b) yet   c) already
12 _____ the invitations yet?
   a) Do you send   b) Have you sent
   c) Were they sent
13 If I pass my test, _____ take you out to celebrate.
   a) I'd   b) I'll   c) I've
14 I've read the instructions twice, but I'm _____. I still don't know how it works.
   a) bored   b) confused   c) lonely
15 I'm not _____ about that.
   a) keen   b) fine   c) sure

16 In my _____, they should sell the house.
   a) opinion   b) thinking   c) idea
17 It's my husband's new car, so I'm very _____ when I drive it.
   a) amazed   b) confused   c) nervous
18 We're going on holiday tomorrow. I'm really _____.
   a) excited   b) lonely   c) bored
19 I've just _____ my webpage – it looks much better now.
   a) downloaded   b) updated   c) written
20 Hi, everyone. Welcome to my weekly _____.
   a) blog   b) search engine   c) website
21 I _____ her we would be late.
   a) said   b) asked   c) told
22 The tour guide _____ we should stay here.
   a) said   b) told   c) asked
23 What would you do if she _____ her job?
   a) leave   b) leaves   c) left
24 If we had more money, we _____ go on expensive holidays.
   a) would   b) will   c) won't
25 If I _____ the lottery, I wouldn't tell anyone.
   a) win   b) will win   c) won
26 I watched a very good _____ about police in South Africa.
   a) horror film   b) blockbuster   c) documentary
27 Snakes, tortoises and crocodiles are _____.
   a) reptiles   b) mammals   c) insects
28 He's a great _____. I saw his exhibition.
   a) photography   b) photographer   c) photograph
29 You want to speak to Daniel? _____ a moment, here he is.
   a) Hold   b) Just   c) Give
30 Can you hold _____? I'll be with you in a minute.
   a) up   b) in   c) on

RESULT   /30

UNIT 1 Recording 1

1 played, stayed, tried, ended
2 asked, kissed, arrived, talked
3 finished, decided, pretended, wanted
4 studied, happened, invented, stayed
5 walked, helped, stopped, started

UNIT 1 Recording 2

When I was eighteen, I went on holiday with a group of mates to Spain. We had a great time. Every day we went sunbathing on the beach and at night we went out dancing. On the last night, I met an American girl called Amy and we got on really well. We went to a 24-hour café and talked all night. Soon it was morning and we both had to go.

We promised to write to each other when we got home, and at first we did. But after a few months we decided that it was too difficult because we lived in different countries, so we stopped. I started university and forgot about her.

Ten years later, I started a new job in London. On the first day, I walked into the office and who do you think I saw? It was Amy! I recognised her immediately – she still looked the same. Of course, we were both really shocked to see each other. She explained that she now lived alone in London because of her job with the company. Well, of course, we got on really well again and we started hanging out with each other. I showed her round London and we went to museums, concerts and restaurants. It wasn't long until we fell in love! It felt right, so I proposed to her and she accepted! We got married soon after and had our son, Jamie. We're very happy together!

UNIT 1 Recording 3

1 Do you like it here?
2 Where are you going?
3 I come from Italy.
4 It's a beautiful day.
5 I'm afraid I can't remember.
6 Where did you buy it?
7 I'm sorry, but I don't understand.

UNIT 1 Recording 4

1 Did you have a nice weekend?
2 Where did you go?
3 Would you like a drink?
4 So, do you like it here?
5 It was nice to meet you.
6 Let's keep in touch.

UNIT 2 Recording 1

7 syllables: motorcycle courier
6 syllables: foreign correspondent
5 syllables: fashion designer, IT consultant, personal trainer
4 syllables: rescue worker
2 syllables: sales rep

UNIT 2 Recording 2

1 People who work sitting down always get paid more than people who work standing up.
2 The successful people are usually the ones who listen more than they talk.
3 Politicians never believe what they say, so they are surprised when other people do.
4 Once in a while, teachers will open a door, if you're lucky, but you have to enter alone.
5 Great artists like van Gogh rarely live to see their success.
6 Doctors are the same as lawyers. The only difference is that lawyers rob you, but doctors rob you *and* kill you occasionally.
7 Find something you love doing and you'll never have to work a day in your life.
8 The only place where success always comes before work is in the dictionary.

UNIT 2 Recording 3

1 I work on a safari as a guide. I take tourists to see the animals. Everyone thinks my job is dangerous, but I don't think so. Well, I didn't think so until last month. So, what happened? Well, I had a bus full of tourists. There were fifteen of them. It was a beautiful, clear evening and about seven o'clock we saw some elephants. Everyone wanted to take photos, so I told them they could get off the bus for a few minutes. So there we were – these tourists taking photos of the elephants. Then suddenly, the male elephant turned. It looked at us. And I could see that it was angry. So I told everyone to stand still. 'Don't move!' Well, the elephant continued looking at us and I thought that it was going to charge, you know, to run at us. I told the tourists to walk very slowly back to the bus. Then the elephant charged at us. I jumped into the bus and started driving as fast as possible. The elephant came very close and the tourists were all shouting and screaming. But it was OK in the end. We escaped.

2 I was on a safari holiday. It was a really beautiful place, very quiet. One evening, at about six o'clock, we went for a drive in the tour bus. There were twenty of us tourists. Well, we soon saw some elephants. They were drinking at a pool. So we got out of the bus to take photos. Anyway, suddenly, this large male elephant started looking very angry. Then it walked towards us. The guide told us to run back to the bus as fast as possible. So we did. This was a really bad idea because the elephant followed us. Then the guide got into the bus and drove away very fast. We were really quiet and calm because we didn't want to frighten the elephant. But it wasn't a nice experience and we were happy to get back to the hotel that night.

UNIT 2 Recording 4

1 I'm very keen on cooking and I absolutely love great food.
2 I love riding my motorbike. I can't stand sitting in an office all day.
3 I'm quite keen on technology and I don't mind dealing with other people's computer problems.
4 I'm very keen on working with money and I don't like people wasting it on stupid things.

UNIT 2 Recordings 5/6

1
A: On Saturday I went to a conference about the Z-phone, this amazing new technology.
B: Really? I read about that last week. It sounds interesting.
A: Well, everybody's talking about it.
B: And what about the cost?
A: Oh, I don't know. I had to leave before they discussed that.

2
A: Today I was offered a job as a babysitter.
B: That's great!
A: Not really. They only offered me five pounds an hour.
B: Oh, I see. So did you accept the job?
A: No. I'm going to look for something better.
B: Right. What did you tell them?
A: I said, 'Dad, I know the baby is my sister, but I want a better salary!'

UNIT 3 Recording 1

D = David   T = Terry

D: So what do you think, Terry? I put it on this wall because of the light.

T: Um. It's … it's … well, I want to say I like it. But I don't.

D: You don't like it?

T: No, David, I don't. It's terrible.

D: What?

T: It's just black. All over. It's black on black. It looks like a painting of a black bird flying over a black building on a black night.

D: It's modern art, Terry.

T: I know, I know. But it doesn't say anything.

D: What do you mean, it doesn't say anything? It's art. It doesn't talk.

T: You know what I mean. It has no message. I don't understand it.

D: You don't have to understand it, Terry. It's art. It just exists. It's not there to be understood.

T: So why is it all black? Why not white? Or white and black? Or red, white and black?

D: Why don't you ask the artist?

T: How much did it cost?

D: I'm not telling you.

T: How much did it cost?

D: Why?

T: I want to know.

D: It was expensive.

T: What does that mean? What's expensive? Fifty dollars? Fifty thousand dollars?

D: Nearer fifty thousand.

T: Nearer fifty thousand dollars than fifty?

D: Yes. Forty-five thousand. Forty-five thousand dollars.

T: I can't believe it! You bought a black painting … you spent forty-five thousand dollars …

D: I liked it. I like it. No, I love it.

T: It's black, David. Black on black. I could paint it for you in five minutes.

D: But you didn't.

T: You didn't ask me to.

D: I didn't want you to.

T: Has Mary seen it?

D: Not yet. She's away. She'll be back on Friday.

T: Does she know you bought it?

D: No. It's a surprise.

T: Oh yes, it will be. A big surprise! Does Mary even like modern art?

D: Yes. She'll like this.

T: How do you know?

D: I know.

T: How?

D: Because I know what Mary likes and what Mary doesn't like. And she'll like this.

T: I hope so. Because if she doesn't, you're dead.

UNIT 3 Recording 2

1

A: You've reached Danny's voicemail. Please leave a message.

B: Hi, Danny. It's Pauline here. I'm calling about tomorrow night. Unfortunately, there are no more tickets for the concert. I called them at about two o'clock, but they were already sold out. So, I don't know what you want to do. Anyway, give me a call tonight after six. Bye.

2

A: Hi, is Tricia there, please?

B: No, I'm afraid she isn't. Who's speaking?

A: It's Elise here.

B: Hi, Elise. No, I'm afraid Tricia is out at the moment. Do you want to leave a message?

A: Yes, can you tell her I'll be at the station at eight. She's going to meet me there.

B: Sorry, can you repeat that?

A: Yes. I'll be at the station at eight.

B: Oh, OK. At eight. I'll tell her that.

A: Thanks. Oh, and can you tell her that her mobile isn't working?

B: Yes, OK. I think she needs to recharge it.

A: Thanks. Bye.

B: Bye.

3

A: Roundhouse Bar and Grill. How can I help you?

B: Oh hello there. I'd like to book a table for three people for Wednesday evening.

A: Oh, we don't take bookings, actually.

B: Oh really?

A: Yeah, if you just show up at the door, that'll be fine.

B: OK.

A: Around eight is usually our busiest time, between eight and nine thirty. So if you come a bit before that …

B: Great. Thanks very much for your help.

A: You're welcome.

R1 Recording 1

1

A: Hello. My name's Felipe. It's nice to meet you.

B: Hi, I'm Magda. Nice to meet you, too.

2

A: Nice day, isn't it?

B: Yes, it's lovely.

3

A: So, where exactly do you come from?

B: Zaragoza. It's a small city in Northern Spain.

4

A: Did you have a good weekend?

B: Yes, it was OK. I didn't do much.

5

A: So, would you like a drink?

B: Yes, I'd love a glass of water.

6

A: I'll see you later.

B: See you soon.

UNIT 4 Recording 1

1 How much do I have to pay?

2 Can I park here?

3 We must visit her before we leave.

4 We don't have to stay in this hotel.

5 She can't wear that!

6 You mustn't tell anyone.

UNIT 4 Recording 2

I = Interviewer   P = Professor

I: Professor Morris, we're looking at learning and the different ways in which people like to learn, and one of the things we can look at is the type of learner. Is that right?

P: Yes, research has shown that there may be many different types of learner. But one way we can look at this is to divide people into two groups: holists and serialists. Now, most people will probably use both approaches, but often we find people are quite strongly one or the other.

I: Holists and serialists. So, what's the difference between the two?

P: Well, students who are serialists like to study taking one step at a time. They look at a subject or topic and work through the different parts of the topic in order.

I: And holistic learners? How are they different?

P: The holists are very different. They like to have a general understanding of the whole topic. And they find it easier to study and learn if they have an idea of the 'big picture'. They don't worry so much about the detail.

I: Oh. That's me. I think I'm more of a holist.

P: Are you? Well, you see …

UNIT 4 Recording 3

I = Interviewer   P = Professor

I: So, tell me a little bit more about the serialist. You said that they like to learn things in sequence, in order.

P: That's right. So, they start at the beginning, and when they feel they've fully understood one part, then they are ready to move on to the next part. But it's very important to them that they understand the detail.

I: OK. These are the kind of people who always read the instructions before they try a new piece of equipment or machinery.

P: That's right.

I: And what about the holistic learners?

P: OK. Well, a holist never starts learning about a topic at the beginning. They jump around and get lots of information. So, they might pick up a book about the topic and choose a chapter in the middle and start reading there.

I: That's like me. I choose the bit I'm most interested in.

P: Exactly. But a serialist learner will start at the beginning and read each chapter in order.

I: That's very interesting. What about writing? Is there a difference there too?

P: Yes, absolutely. A serialist will make a careful plan of everything they have to write and then begin to research each area. But a holist will read about a lot of different things and have lots of bits of paper with notes. Then they will try to put the different pieces together when they begin writing.

I: That's very true. There is paper everywhere. I think my tutors at university would like me to be more serialist.

P: Yes, that's probably true …

UNIT 4   Recordings 4/5

1
A: Why don't we go to the cinema tonight?
B: That's a good idea. Do you know what's on?

2
A: I don't think you should buy that car.
B: You're right. It's too expensive.

3
A: I think we should organise a party.
B: I'm not sure that's a good idea. We're too busy.

4
A: Maybe you should say sorry.
B: I suppose so. I'll call Louise later.

5
A: You shouldn't play so many computer games.
B: You're right. I need to get out more.

6
A: I think you should study more.
B: I suppose so. I want to do well in the exam.

UNIT 5   Recording 1

1 We were open. We were opening the shop.
2 I was fine. I was finding it difficult.
3 They were right. They were writing a book.
4 It was you. It was using too much gas.
5 She was clean. She was cleaning the house.
6 Where were you? Where were you going?

UNIT 5   Recording 2

A twenty-one-year-old German tourist called Tobi Gutt wanted to visit his girlfriend in Sydney, Australia. Unfortunately, he typed the wrong destination on a travel website. He landed near Sidney, Montana, in the United States, 13,000 kilometres away. This is his story.

Tobi left Germany for a four-week holiday. He was wearing a T-shirt and shorts, perfect clothes for the Australian summer. But the plane didn't land in Australia. It landed in freezing-cold Montana in the United States.

He had to take a connecting flight, but when he looked at the plane to Sidney, he became confused. Strangely, it was very small. And then he realised his mistake. Sidney, Montana, was an oil town of about 5,000 people. It was also in the United States, not Australia.

Tobi then spent three days waiting in the airport. He had only a thin jacket in the middle of winter, and no money. A few friendly people helped him with food and drink until eventually, his parents and friends from Germany sent him some money. He bought a ticket to Australia, where, finally, he saw his girlfriend.

UNIT 5   Recording 3

1 A twenty-one-year-old German tourist called Tobi Gutt wanted to visit his girlfriend in Sydney, Australia. Unfortunately, he typed the wrong destination on a travel website.

2 When he looked at the plane to Sidney, he became confused. Strangely, it was very small.

3 A few friendly people helped him with food and drink until eventually, his parents and friends from Germany sent him some money.

UNIT 5   Recording 4

1 Go along Hemingway Road. Go past The Bellow Club and take the first left. It's next to the Baldwin Bar.

2 Go along Hemingway Road, then take the first right. You'll be on Morrison Road. Go along Morrison Road for about five minutes, past the turning for the car park. It's in front of you.

3 Go along Hemingway Road. Keep going until you reach Carver Street. Turn right on Carver Street and it's the first building on your right.

4 Go straight along Hemingway Road. Take the second right. You'll be on Cheever Road. Go along Cheever Road. Go past the school. It's on your right.

5 Go straight along Hemingway Road. Keep going until you reach Nabokov Street. Turn left on Nabokov Street. Go straight on. There's a river, the Faulkner River. Cross the bridge and it's in front of you.

6 Go along Hemingway Road. Take the first right on Morrison Road. Then take the first left. There's a hospital. It's next to the hospital.

UNIT 5   Recording 5

1
A: Excuse me. Can you help me? I'm looking for the Science Museum.
B: Go straight on. You can't miss it.
A: OK, so it's easy! Can you show me on the map?
B: Yes, of course.

2
A: Excuse me. I'm trying to find the internet café. Is this the right way?
B: Yes. Keep going. You'll see it in front of you.
A: Can I walk?
B: Yes, you can. It takes about ten minutes.

3
A: Is it far to the tube?
B: No. It's about two minutes' walk.
A: OK. So I need to go left at the cinema?
B: That's right. It's easy!

UNIT 6   Recording 1

1 I've known her for ages.
2 They've travelled a lot.
3 He's never seen it before.
4 Nothing has changed.
5 I've worked in other countries.

UNIT 6   Recordings 2/3

P = Presenter	W1 = Woman 1
W2 = Woman 2	W3 = Woman 3
M = Man	

Part 1

P: We're in Manchester, and this is table tennis for the over-fifties. The people who play here play three times a week, so you don't need to tell them about how exercise makes you feel better.

W1: It gives you a great feeling. You feel fabulous. Any type of exercise is good for you, especially when you're my age. It just makes you feel good.

P: Scientists have now worked out that you can live longer if you have a healthy lifestyle. They did some research. They followed 20,000 people for more than ten years, and they looked at the different lifestyles they had. The results are interesting. They showed that people who don't smoke, who do regular exercise and who eat five portions of fresh fruit and vegetables every day actually live longer. These people actually live about fourteen years longer than the people who didn't have such healthy lifestyles. They lived longer and they didn't have so many health problems. Doctors say that even making a small change to your lifestyle can make a big difference to your health. Also, don't worry if you've got bad habits now. It's never too late to start. So, does everyone agree that it's a good idea to give up smoking, eat healthily, and do exercise in order to live longer? We asked people on the street to tell us what they think.

Part 2

W2: I don't know. I don't think it's that important. I mean, I don't eat five portions of fruit and vegetables every day. I don't like them, so I'm not going to do that.

W3: If I go out with my friends in the evening, then I'm going to smoke. Having a cigarette is social. It's part of the fun.

M: Absolutely. I think it's a great idea. Do exercise, eat well, stop smoking. And live a long and happy life. Everyone should do it.

P: The message is clear: scientists are telling us that if we want to live a long and healthy life, we need to look at how we live. So, I'm going to have a game of table tennis.

UNIT 6 Recording 4

D = Doctorv   P = Patient

1

D: Good morning. How can I help?
P: I'm worried about my leg.
D: Your leg? What's the matter with it?
P: Well, it's very painful. It hurts when I walk.
D: I see. How long have you had the problem?
P: Since yesterday.
D: Can I have a look?
P: Yes, of course.

2

D: Hello. What's the matter, Mr Smith?
P: I feel terrible.
D: All right. Where does it hurt?
P: Everywhere. And I can't sleep.
D: Ah. Have you got a temperature?
P: I don't know.
D: OK. Can I have a look?
P: Yes, of course.
D: That's fine. It's nothing to worry about.
P: But I feel terrible!

UNIT 6 Recording 5

D = Doctor   P = Patient

1

D: Good afternoon. What's the matter?
P: I've got a sore throat and a headache.
D: I see. How long have you had the problem?

P: About two weeks.
D: Have you got a temperature?
P: Yes. It's 38.5, so I've taken some aspirin.
D: I see. I think you've got a cold. You need plenty of rest and hot drinks.

2

P: I think I've broken my arm.
D: Oh dear. Can I have a look?
P: Yes. Here you are.
D: So, where does it hurt?
P: Here and here.
D: How did you do it?
P: I fell over.
D: I think you should go to hospital for an X-ray.

R2 Recording 1

D = Doctor   P = Patient

D: Good morning. What's the problem?
P: Doctor, I feel terrible. I have a backache all the time and it hurts when I walk.
D: I see. How long have you had this problem?
P: About two weeks.
D: Can I have a look? Where does it hurt?
P: Here. It's very painful. Sometimes I can't sleep because of the pain.
D: OK, I'll give you some medicine for it. And you shouldn't do any heavy work for a few weeks.
P: But I'm worried about missing work. I'm a builder.
D: I'll write a note. OK?
P: OK. Thanks, Doctor.

UNIT 7 Recording 1

1 She used to be very shy.
2 I didn't use to have a car.
3 My granddad used to give me sweets.
4 I never used to study at school.
5 They used to live in America.
6 Did you use to go to the cinema?

UNIT 7 Recording 2

1 used to be – She used to be very shy.
2 didn't use to have – I didn't use to have a car.
3 used to give – My granddad used to give me sweets.
4 used to study – I never used to study at school.
5 used to live – They used to live in America.
6 did you use to – Did you use to go to the cinema?

UNIT 7 Recording 3

I = Interviewer   S = Susan

I: So, Susan, why do people change their names?
S: There are many reasons. Some of them are quite simple. For example, when a woman gets divorced, she might want to go back to her original name.
I: Right.
S: And, of course, other people just don't like their names. But then there are more interesting reasons.
I: Can you give us some examples?
S: Well, the boxer Muhammad Ali was originally called Cassius Clay. When he changed his religion, he also changed his name to Muhammad Ali.
I: So, religious reasons.
S: Yes. And for famous people – especially actors and singers – they need a name that's easy to say and easy to remember. So, for example, the singer Farookh Balsara …
I: Who's that?
S: Farookh Balsara was the real name of Freddie Mercury.
I: From Queen.
S: That's right. The lead singer of Queen. And, of course, Freddie Mercury is easier to remember than Farookh Balsara. Or Georgios Kyriacos Panayiotou.
I: Who?
S: Georgios Kyriacos Panayiotou is the real name of the singer George Michael.
I: Ah.
S: It's the same with lots of singers, actually. Sting's real name is Gordon Sumner. The singer from U2, Bono – his real name is Robert Hewson, and so on and so on. Now another reason people want to change their name, especially if they are immigrants from another country, is to identify with the new country. So maybe you're from Germany and your real name is Wilhelm. When you go to the United States, you might change it to William. Or your name is Andreas and you change it to Andrew.
I: This probably happens a lot in the United States and England.
S: Exactly. People want to mix with others. And having a name that's easy to recognise and to pronounce helps a lot. Another reason people change their names is to separate themselves from their family or from famous parents. Angelina Jolie's father is the actor John Voight. She was originally called Angelina Jolie Voight.
I: But she dropped the name Voight.

S: That's right. And another reason for people changing their names is that there was a mistake. Oprah Winfrey's mother named her Orpah Winfrey. O-r-p-a-h. But there was a mistake on her birth certificate and everyone called her Oprah.

UNIT 7 Recording 4

1
A: It's next to the bookshop.
B: The bookshop? The one near the cafeteria?
A: That's right.

2
A: You can't bring your bag into the library.
B: So, do I have to leave it here?
A: That's right.

3
A: The exam starts at 9 o'clock.
B: Did you say 9 o'clock?
A: That's right.

4
A: I need to buy a notebook.
B: You need to buy a notebook? There's a stationery shop over there.
A: Thank you.

5
A: Can you tell me where the study centre is?
B: It's on the left as you go out of the building.
A: Sorry, can you say that again, please?
B: It's on the left as you go out of the building.
A: Thank you.

6
A: Where can I find Professor Adams?
B: He's in the lecture theatre.
A: Did you say 'in the lecture theatre'?
B: Yes, he's giving a presentation.

UNIT 8 Recording 1

Maggie and Joe Smith lived in the same house for fifty years. When Maggie was eighty-six years old, Joe died. The house was very big, so Maggie decided to move. She sold the house to a businessman called David Jones. A few weeks later, Maggie was at the hairdresser when she heard someone say that the new owner, David Jones, had found some money in her old house. She contacted Mr Jones. He told her there was $10,000 hidden in the wall. Then he said they could share the money: $5,000 for him and $5,000 for her. She agreed. A few days later, Mr Jones visited Maggie Smith. He had a contract. The contract said that Maggie Smith should agree to accept $5,000 for any money found in or around the house. Mrs Smith thought this was very strange. She didn't sign it. In fact, she took Mr Jones to court. In court, Mr Jones told the truth:

there wasn't $10,000. There was $150,000 in the walls, mainly in fifty-dollar or a hundred-dollar notes. Joe Smith, Maggie's husband, was putting money in the wall for fifty years and he never told his wife. So what happened in the end? The judge decided that Maggie Smith should get all of the money. David Jones got nothing.

UNIT 8 Recording 2

1
A: Hi there.
B: Hello.
A: Do you sell towels?
B: Towels? Yes, we should have some in the bathroom section. It's just over there past the clothes.
A: Great. Thanks very much.

2
A: Good morning. Can I help you at all?
B: No, I'm just looking, thanks.
A: For anything in particular? We've got these new jeans. These are just in last week. Or we've got T-shirts here.
B: Um, OK, thanks.
A: Just let me know if you need any help.

3
A: Excuse me. Have you got any of that stuff for killing insects?
B: Um … do you mean an insecticide? Like a spray?
A: Yes, a spray.
B: Hang on. We should have some … um … give me a moment. I'll just check we've got some in stock. Yeah, we've got this one.
A: That looks fine.

4
A: Who's next?
B: Hi.
A: Are you paying by cash or credit card?
B: Credit card. You take Visa, don't you?
A: Yeah, no problem. Can you enter your PIN, please? There you go.
B: Thanks.
A: Thanks. Bye.

UNIT 9 Recording 1

bigger than
smaller than
higher than
colder than
hotter than

UNIT 9 Recording 2

1 big, bigger, bigger than – The population in France is bigger than the population in Poland.

2 small, smaller, smaller than – Poland is smaller than France.

3 high, higher, higher than – Mont Blanc in France is higher than Rysy in Poland.

4 cold, colder, colder than – In January it is colder in Poland than in France.

5 hot, hotter, hotter than – In July it is hotter in France than in Poland.

UNIT 9 Recording 3

1 I'm lucky living by the sea. Every morning I see fishermen coming in after work. There's always something to do because the sea is always different. Every day you see something different. When I was younger, we used to have parties and sleep on the beach. We cooked fish and listened to Bob Marley, and that was fun. These days I still go for walks every day with my dog. We've seen dolphins here. And we saw a dead whale on the beach once. It was enormous. It was on the beach for weeks.

2 As a child, I played in a tree house in the garden. We were always outside. We invented games and we knew the names of animals and insects. We played in our garden or in our friends' gardens. It was very safe in those days. You could be outside all day. When I was young, we didn't have computers or even the television. And there wasn't as much crime, so we really grew up in the garden.

3 I go hiking and camping in the mountains. You can do that here in the summer. In the winter it's too cold. I think Americans like me enjoy the wild. We like big spaces, big skies. I'm just a few miles from a city, but there are all kinds of plants and animals out here. You can see deer and bears. It's pretty amazing.

4 I work with animals all the time. We have chickens, cows and pigs on the farm. There are a lot of farms around here, so it's completely normal to see animals around. I really like feeding the pigs 'cause they're quite funny to watch. One thing I don't like is getting up early. We do it every day. We get up at five in the morning and I'm always half asleep.

R3 Recording 1

1 Could you help me?
2 Can you tell me where the office is?
3 Where can I find a post office?
4 What time does the library open?
5 When do the lessons start?
6 Is the swimming pool open on Sundays?
7 I need to speak to the director of studies.

UNIT 10 Recording 1

1
A: What's your new teacher like?
B: She's really good. She makes the lessons interesting.

2
A: What's it like living in the country?
B: It's a bit quiet. I think I preferred the city.

3
A: Does your mother like staying with you?
B: She loves it. She comes to stay once a month.

4
A: Do you like eating out in restaurants?
B: I enjoy it sometimes, but I prefer to cook at home.

5
A: Is it much more expensive to live there now? What are the prices like?
B: It's not too bad. But it's more expensive than it was.

6
A: Does your brother like it in Scotland?
B: He likes it a lot. He says it's beautiful.

7
A: What's your new job like? Are you enjoying it?
B: It's brilliant. The people I work with are really friendly.

UNIT 10 Recording 2

1 What's your new teacher like?
2 What's it like living in the country?
3 Does your mother like staying with you?
4 Do you like eating out in restaurants?
5 What are the prices like?
6 Does your brother like it in Scotland?
7 What's your new job like?

UNIT 10 Recording 3

I = Interviewer   S = Sophie   L = Luis
P = Pamela

1
S: OK, right. My name is Sophie Dunston and I'm sixteen years old. Well, one thing I don't like is people using their mobile phones or laptops or other technology at the wrong time.
I: What do you mean by 'the wrong time'?
S: For example, during lessons. Or any time when someone's trying to talk to them.
I: Isn't this normal now?
S: I don't think so. Some of my friends don't even hear their parents because they spend their whole life wearing headphones. I think it's really rude.
I: And how would you stop this?

S: Well, in my school they banned personal technology during lessons and I think it was a really good idea. People can concentrate much better now.

2
I: Luis, can you just introduce yourself briefly?
L: Yeah, I'm thirty-five years old and I'm a waiter. Shall I answer the questions?
I: Yes, go ahead.
L: OK. Well, for me the worst thing is litter.
I: On the street?
L: Litter on the street. People just throw away bits of paper or drop food. But it's also on the tube. I'm a Londoner. I go to work every day by tube and people just leave their newspapers lying around. And all this paper is a real mess.
I: How can we stop it?
L: I don't think you can stop it. The government has tried to introduce fines, but it hasn't worked.
I: What punishment would you suggest for people who drop litter?
L: I'd make them clean the streets.

3
I: If you just give your name and age.
P: All right. My name is Pamela and I'm seventy years old. But I think I'm a young seventy. Unlike most of my older friends, I love technology and I use email every day. But the one thing I hate about it is spam. It is so annoying. I think the people who are responsible should be forced to sit down and read millions of spam messages for six months.
I: That would teach them!
P: Of course it would.

UNIT 10 Recording 4

1 There's a problem with my room.
2 Excuse me.
3 Could I speak to the manager?
4 Could you help me?
5 I'm afraid I have a problem.
6 I have to make a complaint.

UNIT 11 Recording 1

1
A: Have you finished the book yet?
B: Yes, I've already started the next one.

2
A: Have you cooked the dinner yet?
B: No, I've only just got home.

3
A: Have you asked your wife yet?
B: No, I'm going to speak to her later.

4
A: Have you decided where we're going yet?
B: Yes, we've just booked a table at Mario's.

5
A: Do you want to come and play football?
B: No, I've already played twice this week.

6
A: Have you seen Miranda?
B: Yes, she's just left.

UNIT 11 Recording 2

1 I get bored very easily. I prefer being busy, so I'm always doing things. Some people just like to sit down and do nothing. But I can't do that. I need to be active.

2 I feel lonely sometimes if my partner goes away for work and I'm on my own at home. But then I call a friend or my sister. Or I speak to someone who I haven't spoken to for a long time. Then I don't feel lonely any more.

3 I get really confused when I have to do anything with numbers, like check bills or bank rates and things like that. I hate that kind of thing. I do find numbers confusing.

4 I am always amazed by nature – the beauty of nature. You can just stand in a beautiful place and look at it, and it's just amazing.

5 I get nervous when I have to organise a social event – like if I'm having a party or lots of people round to dinner. I get nervous about what I'm going to cook and if I'll have time to do everything.

6 I worry about all kinds of things. Often I feel worried about the world when I see the news and all the problems. There are so many problems in the world and a lot of the time I try not to think about them and then suddenly, I'll start to worry.

UNIT 11 Recording 3

R = Robert   M = Miriam

R: I think they've already changed the way we live. I mean, a lot of people, like me, spend a lot of their free time playing online games – and this has made me a more sociable person. It's difficult to play modern computer games alone. When you start the game, you also join a network of other people playing online, and you can join a team to play with other people around the world. I work as a lorry driver, so I spend a lot of time alone on the road. When I used to play computer games when I was younger, I sat in my bedroom, closed off from the world. Now when I play, I'm constantly talking to other players in real time. Because of this, I spend most of my free time talking to other people with the same interests. I used to be quite shy, but these days I find it easier to talk to people I don't know. So yes, I think computer games are changing the way we live, and it's a good thing.

M: Well, they're not changing the way I live very much. I mean, they're just games, like any other game. I quite like computer games – some of them. There are lots of games I don't like, like the violent games, but for me it's just the same as the other things I do. I mean, sometimes I read a book or watch television to relax. Sometimes I go out for a walk and sometimes I play a computer game. It's not changing my life. I don't spend all my time on the computer. I use a computer for work, so I don't want to be on the computer all the time at home, too. And I think a lot of people are like me. In our free time we prefer to do other things.

UNIT 11 Recording 4

M = Manager   W = Worker

M: The project needs to be finished this week.

W: I'm afraid that's not possible.

M: Why not? Everything's possible.

W: I'm sorry, but I don't think it is. We're working hard, but we need another two weeks to finish the job.

M: Two weeks? Can you try to finish by the end of next week?

W: I'm really not sure about that. There's still a lot of work to do.

M: That's true. But you can get some more staff so we can finish sooner. I'm sorry, but I don't see what the problem is.

W: I'm afraid I totally disagree. The problem is that we don't have more staff. We can't find people to start work tomorrow, so …

UNIT 11 Recording 5

W = Worker   M = Manager

W: I'm afraid that's not possible.

W: I'm sorry, but I don't think it is.

W: I'm really not sure about that.

M: I'm sorry, but I don't see what the problem is.

W: I'm afraid I totally disagree.

UNIT 12 Recording 1

Some lines in films are so famous that people recognise them all over the world. One of these is the line, 'ET phone home,' which Drew Barrymore said in her role as Gertie in *ET the Extra-Terrestrial*, in 1982. This line helped start her acting career

when she was only six years old. It made her one of the biggest child stars of the time.

Another line which helped an actor's career was 'I'll be back.' In a scene in *The Terminator* in 1984, Arnold Schwarzenegger tries to get into a police station, but they don't let him in. So he promises to return. And he does, by driving a car through the doors! Schwarzenegger used the same line again in many of his films. For many people, it's the first thing they think of when they hear his name.

When people think of Robert de Niro, they also remember the famous line, 'You talking to me?' from the 1976 film *Taxi Driver*. This line wasn't actually in the script. Robert de Niro just said it while they were filming and it became the line people remembered most in the film. Sometimes words are connected to the role, not the actor who says them. All James Bond actors so far have introduced themselves with the line, 'My name's Bond. James Bond,' after Sean Connery first said it in the film *Dr No* in 1962.

'Frankly my dear, I don't give a damn.' Now this was perhaps the most famous line ever said on screen. Clark Gable said it at the end of *Gone with the Wind*, in 1939. It was used to show that his character didn't care what happened to Scarlett O'Hara, even though he was in love with her. People thought the word *damn* was a very bad word in the USA at the time. But this just made the line more powerful.

UNIT 12 Recording 2

1 celebration, politician
2 photographer, adventurous, celebrity
3 successful, musician, invention
4 dangerous, wonderful, scientist

UNIT 12 Recording 3

1

A: Good afternoon. How can I help?

B: Hello. I'd like to go on a tour of the city.

A: OK. Are you thinking about a bus tour or private tour or boat tour?

B: A bus tour. Would you be able to recommend something?

A: Yes, we have regular tours throughout the day. The bus leaves every hour from outside the hotel.

B: Oh, perfect.

A: Here's some more information.

B: Thank you.

A: Would you like me to book you a seat? You don't have to. You can just wait outside the hotel if you like.

B: I'll just wait outside. Thanks very much.

A: You're welcome. Enjoy the tour.

2

A: Excuse me. Would it be possible to change seats?

B: Um … let's have a look.

A: Are those seats free?

B: Yes, I think they are. Can you hold on a few minutes until they close the door?

A: Yes, of course.

B: Thanks.

3

A: Hello.

B: Hello.

A: How are you?

B: Fine, thanks.

A: Table for two?

B: Yes, please.

A: Did you book?

B: No.

A: OK, let me see what we've got. We're fairly busy, but we may have something. Just a moment. OK, we've got one free table. Would you come this way?

R4 Recording 1

1

A: Excuse me, could you help me?

B: Yes, of course. What can I do?

A: There's a problem with my key. It doesn't open the door.

B: I'm sorry about that. I'll get you another one.

2

A: Excuse me, could I speak to the manager?

B: Yes. I'll just get him for you.

A: I'm afraid I have a complaint.

C: What seems to be the problem?

A: We still haven't had our main course.

C: I'm sorry, but there's nothing we can do at the moment. We're very busy.

3

A: Could you recommend a good place to go shopping?

B: Certainly. There's a new shopping centre not far from here. Would you like me to order you a taxi?

A: That would be great. Thank you.

B: No problem.